TIMOTHY PA...

AND...

JOHN DAVID ...

# PRACTICAL
# FAMILY
# MINISTRY

## A Collection of Ideas
## For Your Church

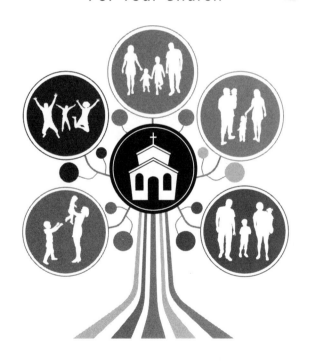

(h) randall house

114 Bush Rd | Nashville, TN 37217 | randallhouse.com

# CONTENTS

# SECTION THREE: DEVELOPING A D6 VISION

## CHAPTER ELEVEN

## CHAPTER TWELVE

# INTRODUCTION

*Timothy Paul Jones*

## THE FAITH-AT-HOME MOVEMENT, WHAT MAKES IT DISTINCT AND WHAT GAPS STILL REMAIN

**I** read my first family ministry book in 2002. My first response was to reject family ministry as a preposterous idea. It took two years for the struggles of ministry and the work of the Holy Spirit to change my mind.

## "I DON'T SEE ANY WAY IT COULD WORK HERE"

Thirteen years ago, I was called to oversee educational ministries in a growing church in Oklahoma. I'd spent the previous three years as the youth minister in this congregation; now, I oversaw the church's youth and children's ministries. A few months after the new youth minister arrived, he traipsed into my office carrying a book with a cover that would have looked trendy a decade earlier.

"I have been reading this book," he said, "and I really think we need to look into trying family-based ministry. This is what our students need." He held up a copy of *Family-Based Youth Ministry* and began outlining what he had learned.

"Well, I really like what you're describing," I said once he had finished. "That's probably the way youth ministry *should* be done. But here? Two-thirds of the students on Wednesday nights come from broken homes, and we just don't have enough intact homes to support a family-based model. I'll take a look, but I don't see any way it could work here."

I read most of *Family-Based Youth Ministry* and then shelved it. I had completed a bachelor's degree in biblical studies, a master of divinity, and a doctorate in leadership—but I had never been assigned a book about family ministry. And so, I did find the book enlightening.

Still, I knew this model could never succeed in our context. If God ever called me to serve in an upper-income suburban church, maybe I would pull this book off the shelf again—but not here, not in this low-income exurban neighborhood, blighted with methamphetamine labs and abandoned trailer houses. When I was the youth minister, I had tried intergenerational activities with mixed success—but there was no way that such an approach could possibly work here as a comprehensive approach to youth ministry.

## CHANGE IN ROLES, CHANGES OF HEART

A couple of years later, much had changed. The church's context was the same as it had always been, but I had recently transitioned into the role of senior pastor. Looking at the church from this new angle, I was concerned as I saw fault lines emerging between generations. What's more, the church had continued to grow, and it was becoming painfully apparent that the ministry staff needed partners to be able to disciple people effectively.

Many factors came together for me that year. One of them was recognition that God had designed the family to make disciples and that we needed to partner with parents to disciple the next generation. I began to evaluate the church's ministries from this perspective, and I remembered a book that I'd skimmed a couple of years ago entitled *Family-Based Youth Ministry.* Throughout the next three years, I implemented more and more intergenerational activities and parent-equipping ideas. I worked with intact families to develop discipleship structures for spiritual orphans. By the end, many of these practices metamorphosed into the patterns I later described in my book *Family Ministry Field Guide.* But, at first, nearly all of my ideas came from a book that I'd shelved as impractical a few years before.

I wasn't trying to be trendy—and I still hadn't heard of any movement toward family ministry. I was simply desperate to draw the generations together and to see children and youth discipled.

It was around this time that I started further doctoral studies at The

Southern Baptist Theological Seminary. Through the texts assigned in a student ministry course, I discovered I wasn't the only one wondering how to partner with parents to disciple children and youth. Chap Clark had already sketched out some rudimentary models of family ministry, "inclusive-congregational ministry" was making an impact in South Africa, and discussions about "family-integrated churches" had already been unfolding for a few years.[1] As I learned more about family ministry, I began to implement more intergenerational opportunities and parent-equipping practices in my church.

In 2007, Dr. Randy Stinson—at that time, dean of the School of Leadership and Church Ministry at Southern Seminary—asked if I might be interested in teaching family ministry. His passion was to make family ministry a part of the training of every student who graduated from Southern Seminary. By the end of that year, Dr. Stinson and I had partnered with leading family ministers throughout the United States, to pioneer a model of family ministry that would become known as the "family-equipping model." It quickly became apparent that family ministry wasn't merely a passing fad; family ministry was becoming a global movement that was bigger than any one of us.

## WHAT MAKES THE CONTEMPORARY "FAITH-AT-HOME" MOVEMENT DISTINCT?

I don't want to give the false impression that family ministry is a new concept that emerged in the late 1990s. Much of what Focus on the Family did in the 1970s and 1980s could be considered a form of family ministry. Charles Sell and Diana Garland were researching and writing about family ministry throughout the 1980s and 1990s.[2] In the early 1990s, the Gheens Center for Christian Family Ministry began publishing The Journal of Family Ministry.

The focus of most of these resources was, however, on the development of healthier families, with foundations deeply entwined in the social sciences. I'll distinguish this type of family ministry as "family life education."[3] The family ministry movement that has gained momentum in the early twenty-first century—sometimes known as the "faith-at-home movement"—is distinct from family life education in at least three ways:[4]

1. **Stronger emphasis on parental discipleship of children:** The focus of family life education had been on promoting healthy marriages and parenting practices; a primary emphasis of the faith-at-home movement has been on the development of discipleship habits in Christian households.

2. **Stronger emphasis on changing church organizational structures to cultivate intergenerational connections:** Family life education tended to work within organizational structures that separated participants according to age and interests; a primary emphasis of the faith-at-home movement has been the coordination (or, in the case of family-integrated churches, the elimination) of age-organized structures.

3. **Stronger emphasis on theological foundations:** Family life education texts frequently began with social-scientific foundations;[5] a primary emphasis in the faith-at-home movement has been the development of ministry models beginning with biblical and theological foundations.

I would suggest that these distinctions have been due primarily to the very different origins of the two movements. Family life education can be traced back to social systems outside the church—nineteenth-century family-improvement societies and twentieth-century social work programs.[6] The faith-at-home movement, however, emerged from within the church. In some ways, the faith-at-home movement seems to have developed as a corrective to the shortcomings that marked many twentieth-century youth ministries: segregation of youth from the intergenerational faith-community, marginalization of parents, and programming that was shaped more by pragmatic focus on numeric growth than by Scripture and theology.[7] Whereas family life education was shaped by systems external to the church, the faith-at-home movement grew from within the church due to discontent with the age-segmented, event-driven programs that dominated youth ministry in the late twentieth century.

## GAPS THAT REMAIN IN THE FAITH-AT-HOME MOVEMENT

Ron Hunter, CEO of Randall House, led the launch of the D6 Conference in 2009. Around 1,400 attendees heard the faith-at-home message in Dallas at that first D6 Conference. Over the next several years, more than ten thousand participants attended D6, and this yearly gathering developed into a catalytic conference for faith-at-home leaders.

As an author and conference speaker, I've been privileged to participate firsthand in many of the recent developments in the faith-at-home movement. Dozens of much-needed faith-at-home books have flooded the shelves during this time. Brian Haynes' *The Legacy Path* has provided parents with an intentional plan for the discipleship of children, with milestones that mark each stage of their growth. Rob Rienow (*Limited Church: Unlimited Kingdom*) and Tim Kimmel (*Connecting Church and Home*) have provided practical strategies for partnerships with parents. Marty Machowski has filled a gap in quality family devotional resources with his books *Long Story Short* and *Old Story New*. My book *Perspectives on Family Ministry* identified three distinct ways that churches pursue faith-at-home ministry; *Family Ministry Field Guide* explored why parents don't disciple their children and how churches can change their culture to equip parents for this task; and, *Trained in the Fear of God* articulated biblical and historical foundations for family ministry.

So, with all these resources available, what else is there to say?

I have crisscrossed four countries over the past few years, speaking to thousands of people about family ministry. In the process, I've glimpsed at least three gaps that still remain even among the people most committed to family ministry—and this book is meant to fill one of those gaps.

1. **The faith-at-home movement has flourished in contexts that are far whiter and wealthier than the world as a whole.** God's vision for His people is "a vast multitude from every nation, tribe, people, and language" with the walls broken down between them on the basis of the broken body of Christ (Ephesians 2:13-17; Revelation 7:9). Yet most of the churches that have successfully implemented family discipleship practices remain white and suburban. I've led family ministries in a multiplicity of low-income contexts, and I am mentoring doctoral students who are studying family ministry models in Korean and Hmong communities[8]—but all of these projects are tiny drops in a vast bucket of need. We desperately need to know what effective faith-at-home ministries might look like in the inner-city congregations, in rural family chapels, in African American churches, among Native American peoples, and with first- and second-generation Hispanic believers.

2. **Parents need to be trained to equip their children to defend their faith in an increasingly hostile context.** Apologetics resources for children are almost nonexistent. Nearly all of the apologetics resources for teenagers are designed to be taught at church, not at home. With the rapid growth of Islam and in a culture that increasingly demands not merely the toleration but the celebration of sexual immorality, children must be able to defend their faith—and the persons who are in the best position to equip children are their parents. Their parents are, after all, the ones who spend time with them day-by-day and who usually hear their questions first. That's why, after the publication of this project and a book on church leadership, I am turning all of my efforts toward the development of apologetics strategies and content to train parents to equip their children to defend the Christian faith.

3. **Churches will slip back into previous unhealthy patterns unless they develop new approaches to support generational integration and family discipleship.** In some cases, churches have spent so many years segregating generations and trying to disciple children without parents that they don't know what else to do. They need ideas for different approaches to the ministries they have

been doing for decades. That is why nearly every week, a church contacts me, asking, "What else can we do in this area of ministry?"—and that's why I've developed this book.

## WHY THIS BOOK?

The purpose of this book is to provide a wide range of new approaches and patterns for each of your church's ministries. Perhaps most important, each of the chapters has been authored by someone who is actively doing what they have described in their chapter. These ideas are structured around what I believe to be the two key dynamics in faith-at-home ministry: *family-as-church and church-as-family.*[9] Before jumping into the ideas, let's take a look together at each of these two dynamics.

## FAMILY-AS-CHURCH: THE DYNAMIC OF HELPING EACH FAMILY TO BECOME A LITTLE CHURCH

The goal of the family-as-church dynamic is to equip parents to disciple their children in the context of their daily lives together. What this means is that Christian households become living microcosms of the larger community of faith as families learn and live God's Word together. Great Awakening pastor Jonathan Edwards described the Christian household as "a little church" and declared "the head of the family has more advantage in his little community to promote religion than ministers have in the congregation."[10] The thought that parents must be primary disciple-makers in their children's lives did not, however, originate in the Great Awakening! This expectation is woven throughout the pages of Scripture (see, for example, Exodus 12:25-28; Deuteronomy 6:6-7; 11:1-12; Psalm 78:1-7; Ephesians 6:4).

Yet, in many churches, church leaders have not equipped or even acknowledged parents as primary disciple-makers in their children's lives.[11] Packed rosters of age-segmented activities coupled with silence regarding parents' responsibility to disciple their children have contributed to the unspoken assumption that the Christian training of children is best left to professional ministers. As a result, Christian parents desperately need focused guidance to know how to follow God's design. Family-as-church ministry contributes to this reorientation by training parents to function as primary disciple-makers in their children's lives. The first five chapters of this book are focused on family-as-church equipping.

## CHURCH-AS-FAMILY: THE DYNAMIC OF MAKING THE CHURCH MORE LIKE A FAMILY

The goal of church-as-family is to help God's people relate to one another more like a family. What this means is that the church nurtures members within a rich matrix of multi-generational relationships. Children and teenagers whose parents aren't believers find their lives intertwined with mature men and women who become spiritual parents and grandparents. Married couples mentor singles. New parents learn child rearing from empty nesters. The entire congregation works together to meet the needs of widows and orphans (James 1:27). Church-as-family ministry clearly recognizes that, inasmuch as I am a follower of Jesus, my family includes anyone who does the will of my heavenly Father (Mark 3:35).

In church-as-family ministry, the church draws people together in a multi-generational family reunion—except that the purpose of this reunion is far greater than enduring a picnic with people we can't stand for the sake of pleasing our earthly parents. That is why the Holy Spirit of God, speaking through the words of Scripture, specifically calls for close multi-generational connections among God's people (Titus 2:1-5). Jesus has bonded believers together by breaking the barriers between them on the basis of His own blood (Ephesians 2:14-15). As a result, those who rub shoulders in the shadow of the cross should be precisely the people that the world would never dream of mingling together—including brothers, sisters, fathers, and mothers from many different ethnicities and generations and socioeconomic strata.

These are not issues of preference or convenience. They are issues of faithfulness to God's design for His people, and they are rooted in the gospel itself. The last five chapters in this book focus on church-as-family ministry.

## THE CHALLENGE OF FAITH-AT-HOME MINISTRY

So which of these two dynamics should your congregation embrace?

Church-as-family or family-as-church?

The answer, of course, is *both*.

This twofold approach is the foundation for comprehensive faith-at-home ministry—ministry that coordinates the God-ordained function of the Christian household with the church's role as a Christian's first family.[12] Alone, either dynamic becomes unhealthy. Together, these two dynamics help the church to leave behind the segmented programmatic approaches that segregate the generations and fail to equip parents to disciple their children.

Church-as-family and family-as-church are radically counter-cultural dynamics. Particularly in Western culture, people cluster together according to peer groups and personal interests, so church-as-family doesn't happen easily or naturally. Parents tend to turn over the shaping of their children's souls to trained professionals, so family-as-church doesn't come easily either. But efficiency and ease are not the goal of gospel-motivated ministry. Conformity to the character of Jesus Christ—the one through whom the first family was formed in Eden and the one who is bringing together a new family even now on the basis of His own blood—is our goal, our purpose, and our ultimate objective.

# SIZING UP PARADIGMS FOR FAMILY MINISTRY

## CHURCH-AS-FAMILY MINISTRY

Equipping parents to disciple children: No

Developing family-like relationships in the church: Yes

Challenge if this dynamic stands alone: Without specific and intentional encouragement to become primary disciple-makers in their children's lives, parents may assume that it is the task of the church to disciple their children.

## COMPREHENSIVE FAITH-AT-HOME MINISTRY

Equipping parents to disciple children: Yes

Developing family-like relationships in the church: Yes

Challenge when implementing this approach: After decades of segmented-programmatic ministry, many churches find it difficult to make the transition to a comprehensive approach.

## SEGMENTED PROGRAMMATIC MINISTRY

Equipping parents to disciple children: No

Developing family-like relationships in the church: No

Challenge if this approach remains in place: With the church's entire range of programming segregated into age-segmented "silos" with separate ministers, parents tend to relinquish their children's discipleship to paid professionals at church, and spiritual formation occurs almost exclusively in peer groups. Neither of these patterns reflects God's design for His people.

## FAMILY-AS-CHURCH MINISTRY

Equipping parents to disciple children: Yes

Developing family-like relationships in the church: No

Challenge if this dynamic stands alone: Without an emphasis on developing relationships with a multi-generational matrix of persons from different backgrounds, church families may become ingrown, focusing only on discipleship within their own households.

# THE FAMILY AS CHURCH

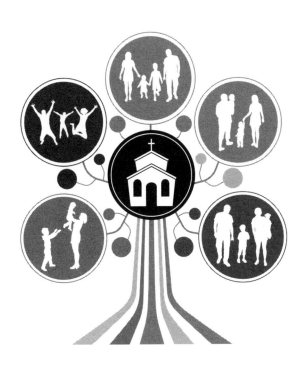

# CHAPTER ONE

# FAMILY, A CONTEXT FOR WORSHIP

*Brian Howard Honett*

I have three boys and one of our almost nightly habits is to read from their Bible and talk about the story. Our oldest boy is almost three years old and is a rough and tumble young boy whom we have taught to protect his younger brothers and ladies. He loves to wrestle and to punch. One of his favorite Bible stories is the story of Creation and the Fall. Almost every time we finish reading the story from Genesis about God's creation and the fall of mankind after the temptation by the serpent, our discussion goes something like this:

Me: "Micah, what did God make?"

Micah: "Everything! And if I ever saw a snake I would punch him down!"

Each reading of the creation story concludes with some sort of discussion that is inevitably a variation of this. We also use the *Catechism for Boys and Girls* and now, even when we are outside and I ask him who made it so hot or any other similar question, the answer is always God or Jesus.

Another almost nightly habit is to sing together. Micah has not yet mastered all of the words to "Jesus Loves Me," but the ones he does know he sings with gusto right along with me. Sometimes this even translates into singing to one of his younger brothers, though often a little too loudly and little too directly in their personal space. He has developed a love of both our Bible reading and singing and if either is neglected he is more than happy to let us know that he cannot go to bed because it is time to read the Bible. Sometimes this is simply a stall tactic, but more often than not God is using his desire to avoid bedtime to remind us of the value of this experience. Nothing warms my heart more than the two rambunctious older boys quieting down on the couch next to me as we read about God's redemption of His people. There is no more sweet sound to my ear than the cry of "One more story, please!"

We are not perfect at our house. The busyness of life and commitments get in the way sometimes. Sometimes I am just lazy. We don't get to family devotions every night, and some nights it seems as if no one is listening even if we do it. That's okay because I know we are trying to be faithful in having a family time of worship, learning from the Word, and praising the Lord together, bad singing and all. When I least expect it one of the boys says something about one of the Bible stories or our talks about it that I thought no one heard.

Family worship may seem like an odd concept. The family is not a church, but there are clear examples and principles that can be taken from Scripture. It starts in Genesis 18:19 as the Lord says, "For I have chosen him so that he will command his children and his house after him to keep the way of the Lord by doing what is right and just. This is how the Lord will fulfill to Abraham what He promised him." There was no local church or synagogue at the time, so it is reasonable to assume that the only way Abraham could have commanded his children to keep the way of the Lord was to teach the things of God at home. We see the fruition of the faithful instruction of Abraham to his family as he heads to the mountain with his promised son Isaac.

Isaac recognizes they are going up to the mountain to offer a sacrifice, but they are missing an essential piece of the puzzle, the offertory lamb. Isaac knew what the worship of the Lord entailed, but where had he learned that? It had to have been at home.[13]

## SO WHAT'S THE PROBLEM?
*Parents Lack a Sense of Urgency*

Most of us would not argue against the idea that parents should teach their children about God. The passage from Deuteronomy has been repeated to us as parents and pastors over and over. Even many unchurched people feel like they should bring their kids to church to learn about God or be better people. The Gheens Center for Christian Family Ministry conducted a survey that confirmed these results.[14] Christian parents know they are to teach their kids about God, and that simply repeating a passage and sending them on their way is not going to cut it. Parents know what they are supposed to do, but it is just not happening. Why? Much of the problem is related to a lack of a sense of urgency.

Parents feel like they have lots more time. After all, the kids are only two, four, or eight years old and there are a lot of years left. The kids do not leave the house until they are eighteen, and they cannot make a profession of faith until they are more mature, so the thinking goes. The problem with this is that the *enemy* isn't waiting. The prince of the power of the air is roaming about the earth seeking whom he may devour, while too many Christian parents are content to let their children wander unattended in the spiritual wild. Those same parents would never take their child to the zoo and allow them to play in the tiger cage, but the spiritual battle doesn't seem as pressing or immediate—though it is far more dangerous than any tiger cage.

Just as the military must act on intelligence warning of an imminent attack rather than risking terrible loss, our churches and families must act on the knowledge that there is an enemy out there seeking to destroy families. It is not sufficient merely to be aware that parents should be leading their children in worship and fathers should be teaching their children the commands of the Lord. Action must take place, and it must take place now!

The glory of Christ's redemptive work is something that children must be learning and internalizing. The goal is not to add one more thing to the checklist of the Christian family. We are all busy enough with school, sports, work, and the multitude of other things going on in our lives. What we need is a change of heart and a Christ-centered life. The outpouring of what Christ has done as parents should spur us to constantly, consistently, and coherently point our children to Him.

## HOW DOES GOD'S WORD PROVIDE A NEW POSSIBILITY?
### *Telling the Story of God's Redemption Through Family Worship*

The most famous passage related to the teaching of children comes from Deuteronomy 6:4-9. We will discuss a lot about the lifestyle of teaching the things of God to our children in other chapters, and there is much more within this passage than family worship. However, family worship is certainly a component of what is commanded here. While the first part of the chapter is certainly more familiar and more quoted when it comes to family worship, the section at the end of the chapter has some pointed words for parents:

"When your son asks you in the future, 'What is the meaning of the decrees, statutes, and ordinances, which the LORD our God has commanded you?' tell him, 'We were slaves of Pharaoh in Egypt, but the LORD brought us out of Egypt with a strong hand. Before our eyes the LORD inflicted great and devastating signs and wonders on Egypt, on Pharaoh, and on all his household, but He brought us from there in order to lead us in and give us the land that He swore to our fathers.

The LORD commanded us to follow all these statutes and to fear the LORD our God for our prosperity always and for our preservation, as it is today. Righteousness will be ours if we are careful to follow every one of these commands before the LORD our God, as He has commanded us'" (Deuteronomy 6:20-25).

Parents need to be able to tell their children the story of God's redemption. The same story told by the Israelite parents to their children of the deliverance from the evil Pharaoh and safe travel to a promised land is our story. We have been adopted as descendants of Abraham, Isaac, and Jacob. As co-heirs with Christ, we share Jewish ancestors whose story is not just interesting; it is a part of our family heritage. It is our privilege to be able to open God's Word with our children and to show them God's many works of grace that tie together His redemptive plan.

"He established a testimony in Jacob and set up a law in Israel, which He commanded our fathers to teach to their children so that a future generation—children yet to be born—might know. They were to rise and tell their children so that they might put their confidence in God and not forget God's works, but keep His commands" (Psalm 78:5-7).

"One generation will declare Your works to the next and will proclaim Your mighty acts" (Psalm 145:4).

In Ephesians 6:4, Paul commands fathers to bring their children up in the nurture and admonition, or training and instruction, of the Lord. Paul recognized the challenge for fathers to faithfully raise their children even though both are marred by a sin nature. A natural reaction when raising children, whose propensity is to sin, is frustration and anger. The self-centered rebellion of children can easily tempt even the calmest father to anger. It is only when empowered by the Holy Spirit that a father can avoid provoking their children in anger and instead raise them in the nurture and admonition of the Lord. Paul does not provide us with step-by-step instructions for how to do this. The text does indicate, however, that fathers should provide both instruction in gospel-centered truths and discipline shaped by the character of Christ.[15] In fact, consider the evidence that even Jesus was faithfully trained in the things of God by His parents. Joseph and Mary faithfully took Him to worship, and the book of Luke says He grew in wisdom. The household of Joseph was one that was intentionally led to observe faithfully the commandment that was given to Moses by God in Deuteronomy 6.

There is not only a great history throughout Scripture of men faithfully leading their families in the worship of God, but Christian history throughout time bears this mark. As one example, in 1647 the General Assembly of Scotland actually issued a directive for family ministry that called for family prayer and the reading of Scripture with explanation, so all could understand as well as to rebuke and admonish appropriately for any who strayed. The directive also called for the father to ensure that no member of the family withdrew and that family worship was performed regularly. Family worship was to be a regular part of life in Scotland and was the responsibility of each home, not exclusively the church.

# Starting Points for Equipping Families to Worship Together

| PRIORITY | PLAN | PRACTICE |
|---|---|---|
| You cannot expect your congregation to do something that you are not willing to do. The leaders of the congregation must begin by putting family worship into place within their own homes. These must be homes marked by regular, biblical worship. | As pastors, deacons, elders, small group facilitators, and other leaders, develop some family worship guides and use them yourselves! Remember that it takes time to develop a faithful pattern of family worship. | While it may look different in every home, family worship should include prayer, Scripture reading, discussion, and even a bit of singing (I know this is the scariest part for many people). The exact format is not as important as the content. Family worship should always be Christ centered. His death, burial, and resurrection is the reason we have to worship. The coming consummation of Jesus as King is the reason we have to hope. Our children desperately need to know both their wretched state and the gracious provision of God for that state. It is in this that they will find hope and purpose in a world of mixed and deceptive messages. |
| Church leaders should serve and equip families by producing biblically-based family worship guides. | Often the best approach is a family worship guide linked to the sermon series. This creates opportunities for in-depth discussion at home related to the content presented at church and deepens worship time Sunday morning as well. | As the leadership is implementing family worship in their own homes, the culture of the church is going to need some adaptation. The challenge from the pulpit can no longer be simply a call for obedience to a command, but an exhortation that communicates a sense of urgency. Families must hear repeatedly that family worship is not a simple matter of checking something off their list of things to do in the week to be a good Christian; rather, it is engaging in cosmic battle. It is worshiping the One who will crush the head of the serpent, the One who has delivered them from death to life and made them co-heirs and adopted children of God. This is not another program they should come to or something else to add into an already busy schedule. It should be the core of who they are and what they are doing. |

| PRIORITY | PLAN | PRACTICE |
|---|---|---|
| Church leaders should serve and equip families by promoting solid tools and resources to deepen and enrich family worship. | Utilizing an age-appropriate catechism, written in contemporary and easily understood language, is a fantastic tool for family worship. | There are a number of catechisms for younger children available online for free and without copyright. Something like the *Catechism for Boys and Girls* can be used for most any congregation with a few minor adaptations for context. As the congregation kicks off its commitment to family worship, a copy of this can be distributed to each family. Sojourn Community Church has even adapted this catechism to include a line for the date completed on each question. This allows for accountability and progress to be easily recognized. |
| Church leaders must strategically build momentum for a sustainable culture of worship within families in their congregations. | The distribution of a catechism and family worship guide combined with a family-focused sermon series will provide tools and momentum to implement a regular program of family worship. | A commitment statement for each family to sign is an excellent way to establish authentic commitment. This could be something suitable for framing and display in a prominent place in a family's home as a reminder of their commitment. Being reminded on a regular basis of the importance of and commitment to family worship will be valuable for the family. Remember that this is going to be a radical change for most families. Few families sit down for a meal and conversation together, and even fewer have the time budgeted for worshiping God together outside of Sunday morning. A signed contract and ready accountability will be vital to make this shift. |

| PRIORITY | PLAN | PRACTICE |
|---|---|---|
| There must be regular accountability for families, especially in the beginning. | Just as you would continue to follow up with a family that was struggling in other areas, leaders must make an organized effort to regularly help those families with their practice of worship. | Families within the congregation should be divided up among the leaders for regular follow-up. When leaders check in with parents to see how they are doing with facilitating family worship, they should specifically refer to the church's family worship guides and recommended tools. Also, be sure to make helpful suggestions for application such as specific patterns for conducting family prayers, and even specific prayer requests. |

## COUNTING THE COSTS OF VICTORY

Family worship is not a program to institute. It isn't just another good tradition to build like Christmas at Grandma's or a big Thanksgiving dinner. It is a vital part of training for battle. The kids will not always buy in. They will not always want to participate. They will fidget and they will whine. It will be challenging at times. That's why we shouldn't suggest that family worship is an easy fix for people's problems or a program that will make everything perfect in their homes. Instead, it is a life-long commitment that will require patience, perseverance, and a long-term perspective. But it is worth it!

I remember when we started making a more conscientious effort to do family worship. Often times it seemed as though I was reading and talking to myself. The only thing that seemed to make any impact was the singing, and only then because they learned some lyrics and tunes. The boys could point out some of the people in their picture Bible, but did not seem to be getting anything we were saying or teaching. Then one day my son Micah came into the room where I was working. I had been angry with him and his disobedience. He asked if I was angry with him. I told him I should not have gotten angry with him and asked him to forgive me. His immediate response was, "We shouldn't be angry because God didn't make us to be angry." This brought great joy to my heart. As we had been reading through Scripture, we continually spoke about God's love for us and the fact that we should be loving toward other people, and that means we do not get angry with them. He was starting to get it! It doesn't always shape his behavior—he still gets angry with his younger brothers when they take his toys, for instance—but he is beginning to understand and internalize what I have been teaching him.

Vince Lombardi said, "Once you agree upon the price you and your family must pay for success, it enables you to ignore the minor hurts, the opponent's pressure, and the temporary failures."[16] To make family worship an enduring practice in your home takes a commitment to paying a price. It means other things (e.g., television shows, meetings, games) must be given up in order to create the time to worship together. It means that parents must be willing to sacrifice time and energy for the purpose of preparing for family worship. Such a price, however, is so small when the eternal implications and benefits are taken into consideration. Just as a soldier considers the steep price of training to be worthwhile as a preparation for life-and-death combat, parents must be willing to train spiritually at home for endurance and success in cosmic battle. May we as church leaders commit ourselves to equipping families to this end until Christ claims His final victory.

# CHAPTER TWO

# FAMILY, A CONTEXT FOR EVANGELISM

*Steve Wright*

father asked me if I would meet with him about his son's interest in becoming a Christian. I was excited to meet with this dad who shared with me that his son wanted to become a Christian so he could take communion with their family on Sunday mornings. I asked the dad if there were any other indicators that lead him to believe his son was prepared to make this kind of decision. The dad said no, this request was the first and only one, and his son mentioned it to him last week because he didn't think it was fair that his sisters were permitted to take communion while he was not. I asked the dad about evidence of conviction of sin, repentance, and lordship, and if any of this had been considered. The dad responded that these topics, including heaven and hell, had been purposely avoided because he did not want his son feeling frightened or guilty. I shared with the dad that I did not feel his son was ready, but he and his wife should consider the practice of regularly rehearsing the Gospel into each of their children's lives. On the way out of the restaurant the dad had one more question which saddened me greatly, "Pastor, do you think it would be okay if my son could take communion now, since we have spoken?"

Two years ago, I was attending a conference for student pastors, and one of the younger pastors shared a story about the number of teens that had been saved and baptized at his church over the past year. I was excited to hear more. My wife, Tina, and I asked him and his wife to dinner that night, so I could hear what God was doing at his church. That night he shared that seventy-five percent of the student salvations and baptisms at his church happened at his church's summer youth camp. Being even more interested, I asked more questions concerning how long they had been doing this and what brought them to this decision. My heart sank when I heard his response: "We came to this decision because we realized if we didn't baptize them at camp, we would never be able to, because most of these kids we will never see again."

Surely saving faith is more than a wafer and grape juice and more than getting a child wet at camp. What about genuine repentance? What about lasting life change? What about treasuring Christ above all else? As parents we need to rediscover the true substance of saving faith. This chapter will consider the role of parents in leading children to Christ, salvation itself, and what Jesus Himself taught concerning children.

## SO WHAT'S THE PROBLEM?
*Parents and the Struggle With Uncertainty, Fear, and Avoidance*

Unfortunately, many parents I talk to feel anxious or unqualified to lead their children to Christ. Somewhere between praying for our unborn child's salvation and answering questions about eternity from the little one lying beside us at night, it hits us: *This is a very serious matter and I really do not want to mess this up.* Christian parents wonder if their child can truly believe, and if so, at what age. Adding to the uncertainty of being too eager or too pushy is the fear of holding a child back. Parents ask themselves serious questions, but are either afraid or embarrassed to ask others for answers. As Cos Davis points out, "Christian parents seem to have conflicting philosophies when dealing with the salvation of their children. Some seemingly manipulate or coerce children into 'praying the prayer,' while others take a completely hands off position."[17] Most parents today are asking, "What does my child need to know and do to be truly saved?"

Fortunately, the answers for the parents' concerns do not count on the opinion of man or the ever-shifting tide of cultural trends. Scripture says much on this subject. In fact, from the first word of Scripture to the last—the entire message of the Bible proclaims the story of God rescuing and redeeming man unto Himself. Christian parents can rest in the promise of the Gospel: Christ has rescued them out of darkness into light, and this promise is also available to their children. In Acts 2:39, Luke records this great news: "For the promise is for *you* and for *your children* and for *all who are far off*, as many as the Lord our God will call."

A clearer understanding of salvation and recognition of what the Bible teaches concerning your children and your role as parent will give you biblically centered confidence. Paul portrays this confidence when he writes to young Timothy, his son in the faith, "[I am] clearly recalling your sincere faith that first lived in your grandmother Lois, then in your mother Eunice, and that I am convinced is in you also." (2 Timothy 1:5). Paul referred to Timothy as "his son in the faith," and Paul was confident that Timothy had a faith that "dwelled within him" (2 Timothy 1:2). In the midst of personal doubt, fear, and confusion, parents can have the same confidence as Paul.

## HOW DOES GOD'S WORD PROVIDE A NEW POSSIBILITY?
*Understanding the True Substance of Salvation*

A proud mom brought her three-year-old daughter to meet with one of our pastors. The mom prompted the girl to share her big news from the day before. Puzzled, the youngster offered, "I went potty." "No, not that one," the mom replied, "the other big thing," hoping to elicit the testimony of her daughter's salvation experience. Salvation can be a confusing thing for children and their parents.

While the technical term *soteriology* can add to the confusion, it really has a simple definition, and it is important that we understand it. It refers to the study of how God has ended our separation from Him because of our sin by reconciling sinners through Christ. In other words, soteriology answers the question: "How does someone become a Christian?" The evidences of salvation can seem overwhelming to Christian parents. Some might find it easier to simply take their child to see a pastor as an easy remedy, but that should not be the default approach. Parents' questions revolve around the fundamentals of saving faith. So what is necessary for salvation? Is it repentance, faith, belief, acceptance, confession, grace, baptism, asking Jesus into one's heart, praying the prayer, or the simple assertion of belief in God? In conjunction with the weight of the eternal significance of their child's salvation, a parent's perceived lack of ability to articulate biblical soteriology in ways a child can understand provides a recipe for the anxiety that many parents feel. Given this, the one most reassuring fact for parents to keep in mind is that salvation is 100% the work of the Holy Spirit.

Christian author Art Murphy, says, "Parents must remember God wants your child in His kingdom more than you do."[18] God, who created us, came to earth and lived a sinless life, died on the cross, and rose from the dead. The Holy Spirit convicts a hardened heart of sin, draws sinners to Himself, affirms forgiveness, creates a new person, and brings about regeneration. The most important aspect of any person—more important than anything one thinks he might do or comprehend—is faith in Christ's work on his or her behalf.

The Bible clearly states there is only one way for anyone to be reconciled to a right relationship with God (John 14:6). "The call for salvation for children and adults is a call to discipleship, to follow Jesus in a complete reorientation toward life, to learn to live for Christ in the world."[19] In God's eyes, children and adults are both objects of God's wrath,

Jesus answered, "I assure you: Unless someone is born of water and the Spirit, he cannot enter the kingdom of God" (John 3:5).

No one can come to Me unless the Father who sent Me draws him, and I will raise him up on the last day (John 6:44).

The Spirit is the One who gives life. The flesh doesn't help at all. The words that I have spoken to you are spirit and are life (John 6:63).

When He comes, He will convict the world about sin, righteousness, and judgment: About sin, because they do not believe in Me; about righteousness, because I am going to the Father and you will no longer see Me; and about judgment, because the ruler of this world has been judged (John 16:8-11).

and we are dead in our trespasses before salvation (Ephesians 2:3-5). "We must never forget that the Bible does not offer one way of salvation for children and another way for adults."[20] Yet salvation is available to all who call upon his name (Romans 10:13); it is a free gift of God (Ephesians 2:8), not based on our good deeds or works (Ephesians 2:9). The hope of salvation that Christian parents desire for their children is strongly anchored in the work of the Holy Spirit that convicts, draws, transforms, and sanctifies. This biblical hope moves parenting beyond behavior modification to the promise of eternity that God has written on the hearts of our children (Ecclesiastes 3:11).

| GUIDING TRUTH | PRACTICAL CONSIDERATIONS |
|---|---|
| 1. Christian parents should be looking for the work of the Holy Spirit in their child's life. | Is there conviction of sin? Does your child understand that his sin is against God (Genesis 39:9, Psalm 51:4)? Scripture never mentions salvation along with "praying the prayer" or knowing certain Bible facts. We must remember that the true basis of salvation, the essential requirement on the part of human beings, is faith alone. One incredible biblical example that demonstrates the truth that the act of salvation is not determined by the eloquence of one's prayer is that of the thief on the cross. Scripture does not record his prayer, or if there was even a prayer that he prayed or if he knew how to pray. In childlike faith, he confessed Christ as Lord. Jesus said to him, "Today you will be with Me in paradise" (Luke 23:43). Anyone in this thief's desperate situation would most certainly do the same. Christian parents should pray that the eyes of their children would be opened to these same truths professed by the thief on the cross. The problem many of us have is that we do not identify our own children with this thief, guilty of sin against God and in need of the same pardon of sin. |
| 2. Christian parents should be cautious about giving their children false assurances of salvation, especially when they are based on ideas nowhere mentioned in the pages of Scripture. | While a child may want to take communion, be baptized like the other kids or even has a desire to not go to hell when he dies, these thoughts may only be the beginning of important faith conversations that allow parents to point their children to the truths found in Scripture. "It is easy to confuse childhood curiosity with conviction. Spiritual interest is a good thing and we should rejoice when we see it, but we need to acknowledge that it is not always saving faith. . . . A particular prayer may or may not be an expression of genuine faith. We need to impress on children that the person who is truly trusting in Jesus will continue to trust and turn away from sin." Keeping the Gospel truths before our children daily is critically essential for us as parents. The response to the Gospel by adults and children alike should be to turn to Jesus as Savior and Lord of their lives in repentance and childlike faith by declaring that Jesus is indeed Lord of all. We must be careful to avoid affirming a child's profession of faith without calling them to repentance. |

| GUIDING TRUTH | PRACTICAL CONSIDERATIONS |
|---|---|
| **3. Little eyes are watching!** | What do they see us treasuring and setting our affection on? Every day our children see us get on the "treadmill of life." What do they see us, their parents, running after? There is a temptation to think that our role spiritually is to take our children to church so the professionals can take care of the spiritual stuff. This line of thinking is faulty and simply will not work in building faith that will last in our children. More importantly, this spiritual drop-off philosophy isn't biblical. It is abundantly clear in Scripture that God intends for parents to live out the Gospel everyday in front of their children (Deuteronomy 6:4-9; Psalm 78; Colossians 3:20-21; 2 Timothy 1:5). |
| **4. The Gospel is for you and me, for our children, and also for the nations (Acts 2:39; Mark 13:10; Matthew 24:14; Mark 16:15).** | A simple and profound reality is this: we will teach what we know, but we will reproduce who we are. If we wanted our children to treasure the Gospel, we need to be on mission and invite our children to be on mission with us. There are many who have never heard the name of Christ; there are orphans; there are children who are hungry and thirsty. The Gospel requires a faith that is missional (Matthew 25:31-46). Neither a believer's life nor a Christian family should be about the accumulation of temporal possessions, safety at all costs, or pretending that our child is destined to be a professional athlete or the next Einstein (Luke 12:15). One of the greatest and most powerful ways to model the Gospel before our children is when we model a radical abandonment of those things that are fleeting and fading in order to embrace that which is eternal. The point and challenge here is simple: do our children witness daily that we really believe the clear teaching of Scripture that says the souls of men and women will spend eternity either in heaven or hell? If you and I really believe Christ's words, then we will lead our families to be on mission. |

| GUIDING TRUTH | PRACTICAL CONSIDERATIONS |
|---|---|
| 5. The central theme of Jesus' teaching concerning children is the significance of their faith and their souls rather than their life stage. | Because our children's souls last for eternity, our clear priority should be set on them coming into the family of faith. Jesus taught that children can possess a faith required for salvation. My children began to ask questions concerning faith at an early age. Tina and I did not feel that we needed to rush the process, but rather saw these questions as opportunities to instruct our children. When they asked about baptism we asked them what they thought it represented. When they asked about the Lord's Supper we asked what they thought the elements meant. These times became meaningful conversations as we talked about Christ as a substitute for our sins, repentance of sin, faith, forgiveness, eternity, and salvation. When each of our three children came to Christ through faith, Tina and I both believed with confidence that we were witnessing authentic faith and repentance. |
| 6. Salvation is not a one-time conversation. | The human heart desires assurances from things we can see, do, or feel. Again, salvation that leads to regeneration is much more than a simple, repeated prayer. This is why we must be very cautious in providing false assurances to our children on things that aren't directly stated or given in Scripture. What we should be watching for along the way is repentance (Matthew 3:8), treasuring Christ (Luke 12:21), confessing Jesus as Lord (Romans 10:9-10), and faith in Christ alone (Ephesians 2:9). |

## GUIDING TRUTHS AND PRACTICAL CONSIDERATIONS REGARDING A CHILD'S SALVATION

God has set eternity into the heart of man (Ecclesiastes 3:11). This eternal truth constantly emphasizes, empowers, and validates our privilege as parents. Eternity is written into the heart of our children as well. This is why Jesus said, "I assure you, unless you are converted and become like children, you will never enter the kingdom of heaven" (Matthew 18:3). Why are parents commanded to talk to their children about spiritual truths? The message of the Bible is eternal, and God gave parents a great role to play in speaking that message into children's lives. As Christian parents, God has entrusted the care of our child's soul to our care! Both Old and New Testaments proclaim the incredible responsibility and privilege that God has given to parents (Deuteronomy 6; Psalm 78:4-7; Ephesians 6:4). Considering the fact that the home is the most formative influence in the lives of children, the ability to share our faith in Christ with our child at home is the most humbling and exciting opportunity we can possibly be afforded as parents.

## Trusting the Gospel Alone

As parents we realize that only the Gospel can restore our children into a right relationship with their Creator; only the Gospel can pardon sin and bring forgiveness to our children, and only the Gospel can rescue the souls of our children for eternity. Every Christian parent realizes that only Jesus holds the keys to eternity. "I give them eternal life," he said (John 10:28). Tina and I both felt the weight of this responsibility at the birth of our three children. We knew at that instance that we held immortality in our hands, and that without God's grace and guidance, we were in big trouble. As parents, we are not alone with our feeling of inadequacy. Our hopes do not lie within our own desire that our children are saved or in our own strength. Our hope is in the promise of the Gospel: "For the promise is for *you* and for *your children*, and for *all who are far off*, as many as the Lord our God will call" (Acts 2:39, emphasis mine). Parents are the first missionaries their children will ever see and for many children perhaps the only living Gospel example these little ones can visibly observe every day. Thank God that His Word gives us the tools, conviction, and confidence to share Christ with our children. And thank God for our children; they are a blessing from the Lord (Psalms 127:3).

Jesus spoke of children five times during His public ministry. Two of these times they were not the primary subject (Matthew 7:11; Luke 11:13), but the three other occasions tell us a great deal that we can learn. Consider these declarations made by Christ about children.

- **Children possess a faith that Jesus said is a model for saving faith** (Matthew 19:13-15; Mark 10:13-16; Luke 18:15-17). Jesus' statements are clear. "Then Jesus said, "Leave the children alone, and don't try to keep them from coming to Me, because the kingdom of heaven is made up of people like this" (Matthew 19:13-15).

- **Jesus said we should become like children if we want to be truly great** (Matthew 18:1-5; Mark 9:33-37; Luke 9:46-48). "I assure you," He said, "unless you are converted and become like children, you will never enter the kingdom of heaven" (Matthew 18:3). Jesus ascribes greatness to those who emulate the humility of children.

- **Children are a gift** (Matthew 18:6; Mark 9:42; Luke 17:1-2). Jesus' teaching in these passages comes with one of his most stern warnings, showing the priority of the soul. We see that Jesus honored children because their souls are of great value.

# CHAPTER THREE

# FAMILY, A CONTEXT FOR DISCIPLESHIP

*John Ellis Steen*

I was blessed to grow up with parents who were both believers in Jesus. Their faith in Jesus led our family in all areas of our lives. Our family's time, energy, resources, and money were all under the lordship of Christ because my parents modeled their faith to their children. One of the ways my parents wanted to pass on their faith involved a nightly bedtime routine. Every night that I can remember, my Mom, Dad, sister, and I would gather in our family room, sit on our couch, read the Bible, hold hands, pray, then kiss each other and say "I love you" to every member of our family.

As I got older, I had friends come over and spend the night. Even though my friends were at our house, our family's nighttime routine did not change, except that my friends would not join us in the family kiss. I confess that I often was embarrassed. Although I did not look forward to this routine when my friends were spending the night, some of them did. I had friends who would ask if they could read the Bible instead of my Dad. They cherished and enjoyed the privilege of being a part of something so loving and family oriented. When the high school years came, I would become a lot more embarrassed of my family's spiritual focus. All of my friends had experienced the nightly ritual at John's house. Even if they had not personally witnessed it, they had their own ideas of what it was like based on everyone else's description. "Steen Family Bible Hour" was the name my friends called the time my family gathered every night to read the Bible and pray.

The catalyst for the ridicule was any mention of me, my house, or my family (usually around the lunch room table). Next would come verbal comments from everyone at the table about the "Steen Family Bible Hour." They would jest about how you had to read the Bible all night, pray out loud, and say, "I love you." Lastly, to baptize their mockery, the sign of a cross was made on one's chest to ensure that I could feel the full effect of the embarrassment.

Needless to say, this lunchroom banter was served *a la carte*. It was hot and fresh almost every day. Worst of all it was free for anyone who wanted to join. I was put in embarrassing and awkward situations often because the faith of my family was the fodder for my friends.

Were my parents crazy or Christ-centered? Were they over the top with these spiritual exercises or were they obedient to God? I am thankful that they were indeed Christ-centered and obedient to God. This chapter will explore the foundational conviction behind their faithfulness by examining what is written in the Bible regarding the parents' role in the discipleship of their children.

## SO WHAT'S THE PROBLEM?
### *The Church-Home Role-Reversal*

The Bible clearly teaches that parents are given the privilege and responsibility for the discipleship of their children. The reality of the importance of parents in their children's spiritual development, however, is frequently regarded as countercultural and thus shunned. Christian parents who do not understand or acknowledge their biblical role tend to "go with the flow" by thinking that their child's discipleship will be fully facilitated at church through organized ministries devoted to their ages. Although the church may be faithful and effective designing ministries for children and youth, it cannot and should not be regarded as a replacement for parents as the primary spiritual influencers and navigators in their child's life.

God designed the family to be an environment that is conducive for a child to develop properly in all areas. A family provides the essentials that a child needs in order to become who God designed him or her to be. A family, led by Godly parents, will be a place where children are loved, accepted, and belong. Children who are loved by a wonderful earthly father will more naturally understand the concept of a heavenly Father's unconditional and sacrificial love. When we love our children unconditionally, they begin to sense the wondrous accomplished, not because of anything they have done or might do. Children that are reared in Christian homes are also blessed with the sense of belonging. This sense of belonging at home can be translated into the family of faith at church. Although parents have a key role in the spiritual process, they are not to do it by themselves. God has called each family to be a part of the local body of believers—the church.

The best plan parents can have to help develop their children spiritually is to realize the distinctiveness of their role and the church's role, respectively. Spiritual growth and learning necessitates a shared effort put forth within a community. God designed the community of faith to work alongside the family to cultivate children's spiritual growth—but the home will always tend to have the greater impact. Since the spiritual lives of children are most naturally and effectively formed within their own homes, it is crucial for the ministry of the local church to impact and equip families.[21] The church needs to work alongside parents to equip them as disciple makers. This partnership between church and home is supported throughout Scripture.

Unfortunately the two roles in this partnership have been reversed.

The church is often seen as exclusively responsible for the discipleship of young people while parents are only nominally involved. This must change if families are to be equipped to fulfill their roles. A great example of parents and the church working together is found in Titus 2:4-5. Referring to this passage, Charles Sell says, "The New Testament urges fathers to be providers and to teach and discipline their children, and wives to have children and to manage their homes. Paul suggested that such training was the church's concern when he urged older women to teach such things to the younger women."[22] Such a partnership between the church and home, as prescribed in Scripture, promises to have the greatest impact on the spiritual lives and discipleship of children.

## HOW DOES GOD'S WORD PROVIDE A NEW POSSIBILITY?

### *The Home as the Hub for Discipleship*

In the Pentateuch, parents are instructed to train their children. Deuteronomy 6:4-9 gives very specific commands of how children were to be instructed.

Listen, Israel: The LORD our God, the LORD is One. Love the LORD your God with all your heart, with all your soul, and with all your strength. These words that I am giving you today are to be in your heart. Repeat them to your children. Talk about them when you sit in your house and when you walk along the road, when you lie down and when you get up. Bind them as a sign on your hand and let them be a symbol on your forehead. Write them on the doorposts of your house and on your gates.

These commands for parents to nurture their children are referred to as the *Shema*. The *Shema* included the truths about God, which the children of God were to learn for themselves and then instill in their children. The instructions contained within the *Shema* were given to parents to teach their children through their everyday relationships.

This teaching was not just an exercise in disseminating information; it was intended to be a part of their lives, something parents talked about with their children throughout the normal activities of the day from sunrise to sunset. God desired for all of His children to know His Word, be able to talk about His Word, and to live out His Word in their lives. Therefore it was imperative that parents understood, embodied, and taught the *Shema* to their children.

The Lord began with the family as the place of spiritual instruction. It was in this loving environment that God gave parents, especially fathers, the principal task of ensuring that spiritual development would occur within their children's lives. God wanted children to "catch" the faith of their parents as they "passed" it to them.[23] The foundation for children's spiritual growth was without question the oneness of God. This crucial truth of the oneness of God was the cornerstone upon which a child's spiritual development and discipleship could be founded, structured, and enacted. These instructions for parents to nurture the faith of their children were imperative but not intended to be rigid. There were not to be set times of instruction such as with a formalized school. Spiritual formation and discipleship was to be woven into the fabric of everyday living with an emphasis on the Great Commandment. Moreover, the original language indicates that parents were to use every activity possible throughout each day to teach their children the truths of God and the lifestyle of Godliness.[24] The clear expectation of Scripture is that the spiritual instruction of children is to be an all-encompassing way of life for parents, who are responsible for establishing a culture of discipleship throughout the rhythms of family life.

In numerous instances throughout the Old Testament, the people of God are instructed and reminded of the importance of intentionally discipling their children. It is clear from these instructions that parents were considered primarily responsible for creating an ethos of spiritual vitality in their home, which would extend outward to make a missional and even generational impact for the sake of God's great Name.

"He established a testimony in Jacob and set up a law in Israel, which He commanded our fathers to teach to their children so that a future generation—children yet to be born—might know. They were to rise and tell their children so that they might put their confidence in God and not forget God's works in order to keep His commandments" (Psalm 78:5-7).

In the New Testament, children were shown to be valuable to Jesus. He touched, healed, and loved them. In Mark 10:13-16 as children were brought to Jesus, He welcomes them, He uses their simple faith as a way to teach others, and He blesses them. Jesus' ministry with children reinforces their significance. In a world where children were devalued, Jesus holds them up as models of dependence and faith.

Jesus' followers taught the importance of the spiritual development of children in families. Paul put forth the home as the chief disciple-making hub. Paul's letters describe and prescribe normative patterns for family relationships, and instruct how families can function properly according to God's standards. The clearest explanation of the roles and responsibilities for members of a household are found in Ephesians chapters 5 and 6.

Christian leaders and pastors throughout the centuries have continued to uphold the centrality of the home in the formation of spiritual truths for children. For example, John Chrysostom referred to the family as a "sacred community." For him, this means that parents should read the Bible to their children, pray with them, and exemplify a Godly way of life. Additionally, according to Chrysostom, a telltale mark of the family as a sacred community is compassion and care for those who are poor and needy. The great leader of the Protestant Reformation, Martin Luther, held parents responsible for the spiritual nurturing of their children. Luther understood parents to be the principal agent God uses for children to receive the Word of God.[25]

# KEEPING THE SPIRITUAL FOCUS IN YOUR FAMILY

The call of every Christian parent is to lead his or her children spiritually. There are some parents who are excited about this task and some who are nervous. No matter how you feel as a parent, you must understand that the Bible sets you apart as the primary and most strategic spiritual influencer in the lives of your children. Although it may seem to be a daunting and impossible task, it can be accomplished. The spiritual lives of children will be enriched when their parents keep their spiritual FOCUS.

> Jonathan Edwards had this to say about the family as a sacred community: "Every Christian family ought to be as it were a little church consecrated to Christ and holy influenced in government by his rules. Family education and order are some of the chief means of grace. If these fail, all other means are likely to prove ineffectual."

## F

**First Seek Him
(Matthew 6:33)**

Parents must keep their own spiritual lives on track. Of course I do not mean they live a perfect life because that is not realistic. No one can live a perfect life, but we as parents must strive for Christlikeness. We can exercise spiritual disciplines in order to continue to breathe life into our own discipleship. We cannot lead our children where we have not been. We must keep alert and alive spiritually so we can be attuned to what God is teaching us so we can pass it on to our children. This process is similar to what is said on an airplane. The airline attendant explains that in case of emergency the oxygen mask will deploy from the ceiling. Next he or she announces that if you are traveling with children, please put the mask on yourself first so you can be alert and alive in order to help your children with their mask. Parents, we need to use our "spiritual oxygen masks" first. We daily need to be reading the Word and praying. Strengthening our spiritual lives enable us to effectively disciple our children.

# O

**Opportunities Come
Knocking—
Listen for Them!
(Ephesians 5:16)**

Parents, there are opportunities all around you that can serve to impact your child's spiritual life if you will recognize and capitalize on them. Unfortunately, our calendars are so filled up with activities that sometimes we do not allow time for the divine appointments and teachable moments that God has placed before us. God inserts people and situations in our paths daily for His purposes, if only we are not too busy to see them. It may be the time we have driving our children to school. We can sing a worship song or share a passage of Scripture we read that morning. When school is finished and the kids are in the car or at home, we can ask about school. There are times that children really want to share something, but they remain silent until they are "quizzed." Some opportunities come once a year. We can celebrate spiritual markers such as salvation, baptism, a call to ministry, wedding, and more with our children. Children love to have fun. Parents, make your family's spiritual milestones occasions to celebrate. Whether it is your spiritual birthday or your child's, make it a big deal. Salvation is an opportunity to party; the angels sure did the day of your salvation (Luke 15:10). When we practice "listening" for opportunities, we can hear many more. For instance, our children are watching how we act and react to the service people that come to our house. Do we engage them? Are we courteous and friendly? Are we trying to build a relationship with them so we might have the opportunity to share the gospel with them? Our children are listening to what we say and watching what we do with all the people God brings into our lives.

# C

**Color Outside the
Lines**

Spiritual growth does not have to always occur while reading your Bible with your children. Think creatively regarding ways to shape your children's spiritual lives. If you are eating at a restaurant, strike up a conversation with your server, invite them to church, or share the gospel with them. Warning: this could be addictive to your children! I have practiced this for years (because my Mother modeled it for me) even though many times I have not "felt" like talking with the server. Often, however, my kids will ask me to ask the server if they love Jesus. Go outside and make a difference. Take a bike ride with your children. Talk with them about God's creation, the fall, sin, and Jesus. It is all right there. Use the backyard play time as an outreach. We share with our neighbors while playing together. Host a block party for your street or neighborhood in order to meet your neighbors. If you have new neighbors, bake some brownies and take them to their house, introduce yourself, and invite them to your church.

# U

**Understand that Your Children do not Always Understand the Things of God**

Your children are on a spiritual journey. They are in different stages along the way based on their age, experience, and exposure to the gospel. Allow your children the freedom to ask you questions. One time our oldest daughter came home from elementary school and asked us what a certain word meant that she had heard that day. It was a curse word. We did not act shocked. We knew she did not understand the meaning of the word. She had just heard it at school and genuinely wanted to know why a friend would say it. It was a great teachable moment about how we can honor Christ with our lips and lifestyle. Talk with your children about money and how you give because God wants us to be good stewards of His possessions. Encourage your children in their "baby" steps of faith no matter what they look like (or sound like).

# S

**Simple Teaching and Activities are Important**

Parents may think they have to get the biggest coffee table Bible (or perhaps the latest hip downloadable version) to make a big spiritual difference. Well, this does not have to be the case. You can do a lot of simple acts to ensure that your children are heading in the right direction spiritually. You can get up, eat breakfast with your children, and do a short devotion with them before they leave for school. If your children are engaged in age-graded ministries at church, ask them what they learned in Sunday School or children's worship. If your children bring activity sheets or crafts home with them from church, take time to discuss the biblical truth contained in it. Develop the habit of asking a meaningful blessing at mealtimes and allow different children to say it. When you make their lunch, put a verse of Scripture on a piece of paper and insert it into their lunchbox. At bedtime read the Bible as a family, pray for lost neighbors and friends. You can do this!

# THE STEEN FAMILY BIBLE HOUR 2.0

I did not begin to appreciate the faith of my parents until after my own salvation as a freshman in college at Auburn University. A friend asked me, "Do your parents love Jesus?" I began sharing about my parents and growing up in their home. I had never verbalized my parents' commitments to the Lord before with anyone (not even to myself). As I sat there talking about my Mom and Dad, I began to understand that their faith had been influencing me long before I knew it. They always took us to Sunday School, church on Sunday morning and night, Wednesday night youth activities, Vacation Bible School, Youth Camp, and more. They always wrote the tithe check first because my Mom said she did not want to die owing God any money. They read the Bible to their children *every* night. They faithfully served at the church in various capacities. My parents wove spirituality into their children's lives every day. I hope that my parents' lives can serve as an encouraging example and a challenging reminder of the duty we have to instill spirituality into our own children's lives.

The seed that my parents planted in me took root nineteen years later. As I look back, I am now proud of my spiritual heritage, but I am embarrassed to think I did not appreciate what my parents were doing then. They were consciously, consistently, and daily investing in my spiritual growth. They kept their spiritual F.O.C.U.S. so that my sister and I would have an example to see and later one to follow. I have begun my own version of the "Steen Family Bible Hour" with my family. I hope this bedtime ritual will have the same spiritual impact in my own children's lives as it did in mine. Investing in the spiritual formation of your children does not have to be burdensome. It just needs to be done, and it needs to be done by you, their parents.

# CHAPTER FOUR

# FAMILY MEALS, A PLACE OF SPIRITUAL NOURISHMENT

*Matthew Scott Thompson*

Growing up, I can remember my mom's home cooking at almost every meal. The table was covered with various piping hot vegetables and some type of delicious meat. My dad, mom, brother, and I would all gather around the kitchen table, say the blessing, and eat together as a family. No particular conversation that happened at the table sticks out in my mind, but the memory of a family meal still lingers to this day. Many years later, my wife, Torey, and I had a little bit of a different approach. We enjoyed spending time together, and in particular we enjoyed watching movies together. When it came to mealtime, our idea of a balanced meal was balancing the food on our laps while we watched the television. We had our mealtime ritual down to an art, we prayed before starting the movie, and when the "amen" had been said it was time for the food and film. Occasionally, Torey and I would take a break if we did not have time for a movie or show, and sit at the kitchen table while eating.

Eating family meals around the television was the normal pattern for our household, which was odd because neither one of us grew up eating around the television. As our marriage grew and we matured, we really began to develop plans and ideas for what we would like for our family to look like. We wanted our family to eat around the family table. The problem we recognized is that we must model *then* what we intended to become a sustained pattern in our family with children *one day*. We couldn't expect to change from eating in front of the television to eating at the table overnight, once we had children. Torey and I took steps to correct this behavior by being more intentional about setting aside mealtime as an important time to worship God through various means, including meal times. Some may look at mealtimes as just another time of nourishment, but I have become convicted and convinced that mealtimes as a family, before and after children, represent strategic discipleship moments where a family can grow closer to God and to each other.

## SO WHAT'S THE PROBLEM?
### *Families Lack Intentionality at Mealtime*

Who would have guessed that eating a meal could be used as ministry? The family meal is an important tool of family ministry. The mealtime is a time where everyone can be gathered together and united for the same purpose. The idea of sitting down to a meal as a family is foreign or nearly impossible for some Christian families due to overly busy schedules. For others, the problem is not the lack of ability to have a gathered meal, but rather that they have not considered how to capitalize on mealtime as an opportunity for worshipful connection and ministry as a family. It is not enough just to occupy common space, eat common food, and simply coexist. There has to be intentionality behind the family meal. In a culture in which precious little of the family is held sacred, a family meal is one simple but profound means of protecting, equipping, and ministering to your family.

## HOW DOES GOD'S WORD PROVIDE A NEW POSSIBILITY?

### Biblical Foundations and Priorities for Family Meals

What does the word of God say about mealtime? Meals in the Old Testament were used for more than just to nourish the human body. God in His sovereignty created and intended meals to glorify Himself. Paul instructs the Corinthians in all that they do they are to glorify God, even in what they eat or drink (1 Corinthians 10:31). Nothing from food to the major events of life should be seen in any other light than that of serving a purpose to glorify Him. Let's explore some biblical examples of gathered meals in order to arrive

Perhaps an important starting point is to think about the concept and purpose of a meal. Today, meals are typically seen as quick moments to fuel our bodies in order to accomplish the many tasks that we have in our busy lives. The more quickly we can make a meal, the more time we will have for other things. I confess I am guilty of devouring my food like a caged animal that has not eaten in years so I can move on to whatever is next that I have deemed more significant. Some people use meals to seal business deals, to bribe others, or to merely enjoy the consumption of food. We can all agree that meals exist to set aside times of nourishment for our bodies, but they are more purposeful than that. Mealtimes were intentionally designed to allow for worship, fellowship, and ministry.

at some practical applications regarding how parents can redeem the family meal as family ministry.

The overarching purpose of meals or feasts in Scripture was primarily a part of worship and devotion to God. God is holy, and demands holiness in everything, including meals. In fact, God has ordained and instituted meals or feasts Himself. God purposed meals to be a reminder of His character and His deeds. The first major feasts established were the Passover meal and the Feast of the Unleavened Bread. These meals or feasts were not put into place for dietary fulfillment, but for the expression of something greater—something eternally significant. Each feast centered on elements that were used to worship God and to instruct future generations in the history of

God's people, the worship of God, and obedience to God. God makes this idea very clear when He commands the Israelites in Exodus 12:17 saying, "You are to observe the Festival of Unleavened Bread because on this very day I brought your divisions out of the land of Egypt. You must observe this day throughout your generations as a permanent statute." God designed the mealtime to replenish and refuel the body, but more importantly He designed the meal to foster worship as it pointed to who He is and what He does. Scripture gives us four purposeful, applicable categories related to gathered meals that can reframe our perspective regarding the ministry of mealtime: discipleship, fellowship, service and evangelism, and prayer.

*First, family meals should serve the purpose of family ministry as an avenue for discipleship and teaching.* Everything is for the worship of God, and through family meals the family can be discipled through fellowship, prayer, and teaching. Discipleship is the centerpiece of the church's work. Most church ministries are centered on programmatic discipleship. In programmed discipleship, what is often missed is the value of the organic flow of life as opportunities for spiritual growth. One of those opportunities is the meal. Jesus was the master discipler at mealtime. More than twenty times throughout the gospels, Jesus is recorded teaching someone over some type of a meal. The only miracle to be recorded in all four Gospel accounts is the feeding of the five thousand (a meal).

Perhaps the most prominent teaching moment over a meal occurs when Jesus establishes the Lord's Supper (Matthew 26:17-30; Mark 14:12-24; Luke 22:7-23). Matthew records the event in this way,

> "As they were eating, Jesus took bread, blessed and broke it, gave it
> to the disciples, and said, "Take and eat it; this is My body." Then
> He took a cup, and after giving thanks, He gave it to them and said,
> "Drink from it, all of you. For this is My blood that establishes the
> covenant; it is shed for many for the forgiveness of sins. But I tell you,
> from this moment I will not drink of this fruit of the vine until that
> day when I drink it in a new way in My Father's kingdom with you"
> (Matthew 26.26-29).

Jesus reinterprets the Passover meal to teach the disciples about who He is and what He came to do. This was the reference to the new covenant, which was about to begin.[26] The symbolism of the meal was already present, but Christ took that moment to raise the standard of the symbolism in the meal to point to Himself. Jesus used the meal as an intentional time to fellowship with His disciples, and more importantly, to also teach them important truths during this intimate mealtime. Jesus taught the disciples in various ways and places, and He used the mealtime as a prime opportunity to teach His disciples about the Word of God.

*Second, family meals should serve the purpose of family ministry as an avenue for enriching and transformative fellowship.* Some of my greatest memories were the Sunday fellowship meals we would have after church. Not only was there great food lined on several tables, there were people packed in the fellowship hall, shoulder to shoulder as they ate, talked, laughed, and bonded over a meal. Eating a family meal together displays and communicates a sense of authentic community. Throughout Scripture and in the early church, mealtime was associated with fellowship and community.

The believers had everything in common, even meals. Meals were more about community and fellowship as they ate and praised God through eating. Their theology and love for God extended out into their love for each other. Their meal times were more than just a Sunday School class or small group social, it was about God and what He was doing

> ### KEY TRUTHS
>
> "And they devoted themselves to the apostles' teaching, to the fellowship, to the breaking of bread, and to the prayers. . . . Now all the believers were together and held all things in common. . . . Every day they devoted themselves to meeting together in the temple complex, and broke bread from house to house. They ate their food with a joyful and humble attitude, praising God and having favor with all the people. And every day the Lord added to them those who were being saved" (Acts 2:42, 44, 46-47).

through the body of believers. As a result of all of this, God added to their numbers.

*Third, family meals should serve the purpose of family ministry as an avenue for service and evangelism.* Jesus used meals in Scripture to reveal things and teach things about Himself and God. One key aspect of His approach was the guests He invited. Jesus ate with a wide array of people from Pharisees to tax collectors to social outcasts. Matthew received his call from Jesus in the context of a meal:

> While He was reclining at the table in Levi's house, many tax collectors and sinners were also guests with Jesus and His disciples, because there were many who were following Him. When the scribes of the Pharisees saw that He was eating with sinners and tax collectors, they asked His disciples, "Why does He eat with tax collectors and sinners?" When Jesus heard this, He told them, "Those who are well don't need a doctor, but the sick do need one. I didn't come to call the righteous, but sinners" (Mark 2:15-17).

The Pharisees were appalled that Jesus would lower Himself to dine with such a crowd of people. Jesus knew the kind of people with whom He was eating, and He did so intentionally. In fact, this was the character of Jesus' mission.[27] He told the Pharisees that the vilest of sinners was who needed Him, not the righteous. Jesus used a meal to identify with those whom He was trying to reach. He made a bold statement about extending the boundaries at the table of fellowship. Jesus was offering peace and reconciliation with God for the people who would never be offered the good news anywhere else.[28] No longer was it just the Jews or the religious leaders who were welcome at the table, but Christ extended the boundaries through His work of salvation (Romans 11).

*Fourth, family meals should serve the purpose of family ministry as an avenue for prayer.* One thing that most Christian families do before a meal is pray; they ask God to bless the food. Prayer before a meal was a common practice among early believers.[29] Even Jesus, who was God in the flesh, prayed before He ate a meal. This is seen in the accounts of the Lord's Supper and other passages of Scripture (e.g., Matthew

26:17-30; Mark 14:12-24; Luke 22:7-23; 1 Thessalonians 5:18; Acts 27:35). The term used in some translations is that Jesus "gave thanks." Prayer and thanksgiving are tied closely together. Unfortunately, the blessing many times is overlooked as an important part of the meal. People tend to treat prayer as a ritual, rather than a powerful teachable moment. Prayer is important to the meal because it recognizes God as the provider and source of the food a person is about to consume.

## MAXIMIZING THE MINISTRY OF MEALTIME

| MEALTIME MINISTRY OPPORTUNITY | PRACTICAL APPLICATIONS |
| --- | --- |
| 1. Discipleship | How can you use mealtimes to teach and disciple your family? In our case, though we do not have children, Torey and I often will invite teenagers from our church to our house for a meal. This gives us the opportunity to engage in informal teaching and dialogue on matters related to understanding the truths of God living a gospel-centered life. Also, there are more practical ways to practice spiritual disciplines through a family meal. One of these ways is to systematically read a passage of Scripture before the family prays and begins to eat. The family is together, and what better time to do a family devotion. |
| 2. Fellowship | True fellowship at a family meal requires more than just physical presence. In order for the family meal to work as family ministry, intentionality and discipline is required. When conversing and eating together, families must make an intentional effort to engage one another selflessly. Basic conversation is the first step to producing fellowship around the table. Asking each other about how the day went or exciting events can spark a conversation that taps into important issues or concerns. Learn to ask probing questions about your family members' lives in a disarming and sincere way. When the question "What did you learn in school today?" is asked, do not settle on the surface answer of "nothing." Do not just act interested in your families' lives, actually be |

**2. Fellowship (Cont.)**

interested in their lives. Talk about the things of God. Use the dinner conversation not only to teach, but also to be transparent. Tell a joke, a funny story, or a serious story; the key is to engage in conversation to begin building bonds of fellowship. Do not answer the phone, watch TV, allow texting, or other distractions during the meal. Focus on God as you focus on each other and build those relationships to build up the Kingdom of God. One final thing: let your family know how much you love them at the table.

**3. Service and Evangelism**

Service and evangelism may seem like tough concepts to put into practice through family meals. Perhaps this is not because we cannot find ways to do it, but because Christ is asking us to extend our love and kindness outside the bounds of the fellowship table, even to those who may make us uncomfortable. We are to love our neighbors and our enemies alike. As a family, we can use the family meal as more than ministry to our own families, but also as an opportunity to minister as a family. By inviting someone who is less fortunate, alone, or hurting to our family meal, we are sharing the love and light of Christ. By intentionally hosting non-believers at our family meals, we create a prime opportunity both to speak and exemplify the grace and truth of Christ and His gospel.

**4. Prayer**

Through a time of prayer before a meal, we can demonstrate to our families the elements that need to be contained within a prayer, just as Jesus demonstrated with the model prayer (Matthew 6:9-14; Luke 11:1-4). Within the prayer, Jesus demonstrates calling on God in praise, thanksgiving, confession, and supplication. The blessing doesn't have to be the biggest and longest prayer, but too often we tend to fly through the blessing to get to the food. Prayer allows for a time of reflection on who God is and what He has done, particularly that day. We can teach our children simple truths of Scripture through our prayers. We can also teach patience. Perhaps most importantly, we teach our children to communicate with God

**4. Prayer (Cont.)**

and honor Him in simple blessings like eating a meal. Consider pausing for a few moments and sharing praises, thanksgiving, or requests before dinner.

## *Consumed by Encountering Christ at Family Meals*

Mealtimes are more than consuming food; they are a time that God in His goodness has provided to serve a purpose that ultimately glorifies Him. How is your family seeking to glorify God through the family meal? Families ought to use mealtime as an intentional time of worship and ministry because parents are to be the primary influencers and disciple-makers in their children's lives. Mealtime is a God-given opportunity for growth in Christlikeness that is too often overlooked. Just by taking the time to be intentional with our meals, we can grow in our relationship with God and with each other as we seek to worship Him and further His Kingdom. Families can be discipled through biblical reflection at mealtime. Families can engage in enriching and transformative fellowship at mealtime. Families can be missional with their mealtime by pursuing service and evangelism. And finally, families can come before the one true and living God together at mealtime through prayer. What a fantastic privilege it is to be consumed by encountering Christ at family meals! Let us commit ourselves, as Christian spouses and parents, to redeeming the ministry of mealtime for the sake of Christ and His Kingdom.

# CHAPTER FIVE

# FAMILY ON MISSION

*Scott Douglas*

How old were you the first time you went on a mission trip? Some of us first experienced missions in our teenage years or even earlier. We remember the experience of going to a different place, riding in an over-packed van, perhaps even sharing the gospel with people who had never heard.

But what if your first mission trip took place when you were forty years old?

That's what happened in the lives of Carey and April.

Carey and April were Sunday School teachers in a church that I served. They were deeply involved in their daughters' lives, and they were working hard to raise their daughters to join in God's mission. But then they recognized that, even though they had told their daughters the Great Commission was every Christian's calling, they hadn't shown their daughters the importance of missions.

"Our daughters have grown up in such a comfortable environment and have never really experienced what else is happening around the world," April said to my wife. "We don't want them to take the life they have for granted, and we want them to see how they can make an impact for Jesus. We have done some small things around town, but what we want is for them to get outside of their comfort zone, out of our comfort zone, and see what else is out there."

Carey and April asked if our upcoming mission trip to Memphis might be an appropriate experience for them and their girls, eleven and eight years old. I agreed for two reasons. First, I thought it was a great idea for a family to serve together. The second reason was a little less altruistic: I knew they would be great sponsors, and I needed all the help I could get.

Over the next few weeks, they prayed for the trip and talked to their daughters about what challenges they might experience. They participated in local missions to prepare. Once they reached Memphis, the mission trip was an eye-opening experience for these two elementary-aged girls from rural Kentucky. They saw what urban poverty looks like, and what it means for Christ to be someone's only hope. The activities were simple—serving tables at a shelter, preparing care packages for the homeless, organizing clothing—but God worked through these acts of service to reshape a young family's life.

> Today, Carey and April have taken the lead in mobilizing mission trips for families in our church. They recruited three other families for a return trip to the same location in Memphis. They've reminded us that it's not enough to promote missions in our church. The church is also responsible to encourage parents to adjust their priorities, their schedules, even their vacation weeks so they can engage personally in mission efforts.

## SO WHAT'S THE PROBLEM?
### *We Forget Where the Mission Begins*

The mission field isn't only a far-away place that requires passports and immunizations. Sure, that's one part of missions, and it's vitally important—but the mission field begins in the homes of believing moms and dads as they share the gospel with their children. God designed the family to serve as a primary means for transmitting the gospel and multiplying His kingdom.

But the family is even more than a mission field. The family is also a missions training and sending agency! Families train and send missionaries because missions is about being a disciple and making more disciples wherever God places you. Developing missionary habits in your home now prepares your children to serve as missionaries around the world as they grow. Missions extend around the world—but missions begin at home.

## HOW DOES GOD'S WORD PROVIDE A NEW POSSIBILITY?

### God's Vision for Families Has Always Been Global

God designed the family to fill the cosmos with living reflections of His glory (Genesis 1:28). But it's quite possible that this mission has been buried under a never-ending burden of busy-ness in your family. Perhaps your family is fragmented by an unending calendar of school activities, sports, clubs, parent meetings, and church functions. Maybe, when you think about your family as the beginning place for God's mission, all you sense is discouragement. After all, when was the last time you ate together, played together, or prayed with your children? For that matter, when was the last time you were all in the same time zone?

Might I suggest that missions could be a means to unite your family in a common purpose? At this point, I'm not pointing merely to mission trips. Suppose that you made a particular, local mission the first priority in your family's schedule. What if you committed to a mission effort in your home or community and did something every week to move forward that mission in some way? What might change in your family? Here are a few possibilities:

1. **More communication than before**. Make time to discuss progress in your mission efforts during family meals. Select a project you'll complete over a set period of weeks or months. This might be anything from a particular number of total hours you'll serve, how many meals you'll serve, a number of people with whom you'll engage, or how many items you'll collect and share. Track and celebrate your progress as a family. One result could be that you have more in common with your family members, resulting in richer and more meaningful communication with one another.

2. **Launch of a mission's legacy that lasts for generations**. The goal of missions isn't limited to the work of missions. For my wife and me, part of the goal of missions is to share our love for missions with our sons. We hope as we work to build our family around missions that it would have an impact across our church. We want to see parents and grandparents serving the homeless, packing shoeboxes for Christmas presents, and praying for unreached people groups.

3. **Cultivation of compassion for your community and for the world**. I've spoken to dozens of teenagers and adults who grew in their compassion toward others through their first mission trip—even if the "trip" was only a local outreach, preparing meals for the homeless or volunteering at a pregnancy crisis center.

4. **Renewed recognition of God's purpose for families**. From the very beginning, God meant families to function as outposts of His kingdom work. Families were formed as a means to multiply God's manifest glory around the globe so His splendor fills the earth like the waters fill the sea (Genesis 1:28). Families who place a priority on missions find fulfillment as they participate in God's eternal purpose for families. My point in these four possibilities is not to instill false hopes for a quick fix! In fact, without

accountability and intentional follow-up after mission efforts, it's unlikely that any lasting change will occur.[30] I simply want you to glimpse a few of the fruits you might see when families choose to participate in God's mission in the world.

## PRACTICES THAT PROVIDE OPPORTUNITIES FOR FAMILIES TO BE ON MISSION

| PLAN | PURPOSE | PRACTICE |
|---|---|---|
| Pray weekly for particular people groups around the globe and provide families with prayer guides. | To develop a global vision in families through prayer | A simple way to cultivate a global vision among families is to lead them in persistent prayer for people groups that need to hear the gospel. Helpful resources include the Joshua Project (http://www.joshuaproject.net), as well as http://www.peoplegroups.org and http://www.peoplegroups.info. Through your church, you can also adopt a people group and partner with a missionary who works with this people group (http://www.imb.org/lead/howtoconnect.aspx). In many churches, these partnerships develop into short-term international mission trips. |
| Plan a family-friendly local outreach opportunity each month. | To engage every family in your church in local missions | Plan a monthly outreach in which families can serve together. Some ideas could include a local food pantry, clothes closet, senior adult center, or after school programs. Keep your time commitment reasonable. The key is a consistent lifestyle of serving, not trying to change the earth's rotation! Some families will need to be willing to include "spiritual orphans"—children or students who are part of your church, but whose parents aren't—in their families during these outreach opportunities. |

| PLAN | PURPOSE | PRACTICE |
|---|---|---|
| Equip families to develop relationships with neighbors who are non-believers. | To develop evangelistic habits in families, centered around family meals | Emphasize inviting non-believing neighbors for meals, with the purpose of developing relationships that allow families to share the gospel. Encourage church members to designate one evening each month to invite a non-believing family for dinner. Train church members to seek ways to share the gospel with their guests. One of the best training tools available is the Three Circles: Life Conversation Guide (http://www.namb.net/video/3circlesguide/). |
| Connect small groups and children's classes with missionaries on the field. | To develop a global vision in families through connections with missionaries | At least four times each year, have a missionary record a brief video showing his or her work and sharing needs. Show this video in each small group and children's class. Develop a brief prayer guide so families can pray for this missionary together during the week in their homes. |

## *Adopted for a Mission*

You may find yourself wondering if this task is too big for you to accomplish in your church; if so, you're more correct than you may know. This task *is* too big for you to accomplish alone! But that's why God gives us the church around us and His Spirit within us, to accomplish together through His power that which none of us could ever accomplish alone.

That's also the answer to another concern you may have about this model: What about children and students whose parents aren't believers? And what about widows or singles? These children and students fit into this model the same way that any of us fits into the family of God: adoption. Widows, singles, and spiritual orphans are enfolded into families to participate together in God's mission.

My prayer for our children is that they will grow to love Jesus, to serve the church, and to have a heart for the nations. My wife and I long for our family to be a family that seeks to live on mission, not merely go on mission trips. The greatest joy that I could have with my children is not that we went to football games together or that I taught them how to make a living. My greatest joy will be if they learn to love Jesus and to join in God's global mission. "I would rather my children be on the other side of the world as part of God's mission than next door to me outside God's mission," Timothy Paul Jones has said. "I would rather my children end up in a grave inside God's will than in a mansion outside God's will."

> Family-equipping ministry recognizes that the gospel compels God's people to view every person as a potential or actual brother or sister in Christ. This passion begins with those who are nearest to us— those in our own families—and then expands to include those who are far. . . .
>
> The apostle Peter put it this way during the Feast of Pentecost: 'This promise is for you and for your children and for all who are far off' (Acts 2:39). . . . The promise of the gospel is for those who are near— but this nearness compels us to share the Word with those who are far, so that the gospel becomes near to them as well.[31]

Before you is the choice to lead your church and your families to be on mission. You see them every day, people who without the gospel of Christ are doomed for an eternity apart from Him. God has uniquely set apart the family for missions, yours and mine. Will our families join in God's mission to see the world impacted for the gospel?

How, at a practical level, can families develop a clear vision for how they will be used in God's service and mission? Here is one simple possibility: *Develop a family mission statement.* The precise process of developing such a statement may vary from family to family. The parents in the household, and particularly the father, are ultimately responsible for the content and implementation of this statement. At the same time, this is a process that your family can undertake together.

As you consider the process, do recall that God has already made his central mission clear in the ministry of Jesus: His mission is his own glory (John 17:1-5, 22-24). Rightly understood, any Christian family's mission statement could begin with 'Our family exists to glorify God by . . .' With that in mind, here's one way to begin the process of developing a clear mission statement for your family:

• **Discuss your values.** Ask your family what is most important to each of them and record the answers.

• **Evaluate your values**. Ask your family to evaluate each response in light of Scripture. Rework or eliminate responses that are not in agreement with Scripture. Together, perhaps over a few weeks, pray and reflect on what will become your family's core values.

• **Compose your family mission statement.** As a husband and wife, allow the Scriptures to shape the direction and language of your family's mission statement (see, for example, Gen. 12:1-3, 18:19; Josh. 24:15; 1 Kings 2:1-4; 1 Cor. 16:15). If you have children, discuss the statement with them; clarify your family's expectations based on this Scripturally-shaped statement. How your family will engage in outreach and evangelism should be essential to this statement.

• **Make a family commitment.** Work with the entire family to memorize the family mission statement.

• **Establish a game plan.** Parents—and especially fathers—must take the initiative in planning and setting goals to implement the mission statement in specific ways in daily living.[32]—Michael S. Wilder

# THE CHURCH AS
# A FAMILY

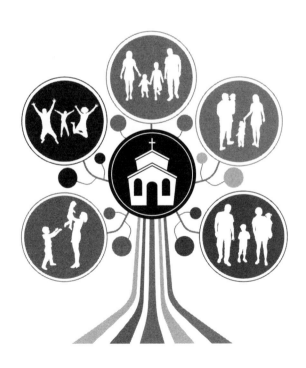

# CHAPTER SIX

# BE A FAMILY BY EQUIPPING PARENTS

*Danny R. Bowen*

Y ou've heard that close counts in horseshoes and hand grenades. I don't know about horseshoes, but I'm living proof that it's true for hand grenades.

At age eighteen, I earned an expert marksmanship badge in hand grenades. After I practiced for a while with cap-filled simulators, the drill sergeant handed me the real thing. I pulled the safety pin, assumed the proper stance—live grenade next to my ear—and waited until the sergeant had mercy on me. Three hours later—or maybe it was three seconds and it only seemed like hours—he gave the order to throw. Unfortunately, when my big moment came, I missed the target. Fortunately, close counts in horseshoes and hand grenades, and I was credited as an expert grenade lobber.

But actually, that wasn't my first grenade-lobbing experience.

I had tossed another grenade a few months earlier in my church.

My assigned task was to follow a leader in our church for a week and then try to step into that leader's shoes. I chose the pastor and his project for me was to preach a sermon. That sermon qualified as my first hand grenade, lobbed unskillfully into the midst of an unsuspecting congregation. Worst of all, this "grenade" didn't land anywhere near the mark.

My sermon topic, chosen after at least one millisecond of consideration, was one that seemed to hold great promise for a passionate sermon: I would preach on the end times. I had read Hal Lindsey's *The Late Great Planet Earth*, so I knew we had a decade or less to convert the world. I had looked at Matthew Henry's one volume *Commentary on the Whole Bible* one time, so I knew I was biblically grounded. When I ascended those steps to the pulpit I was confident that the church was moments from catching my passion. I imagined they would want to leave quickly to make wise use of the short time we had left on earth.

I was right about one thing.

They *did* want to leave quickly.

In fact, leaving became their passion, and reaching the end of our short time together seemed the wisest thing to do. I had great passion but my message had no discernible point. Long before it was over, the few members of that congregation who were not fumbling with their car keys were coloring in the round letters on their church bulletins. That first experience in the pulpit was a lot like my first experience with the hand grenade. I fumbled around and then hurled what I had into the audience. The difference was that what I hurled from the pulpit didn't even land close to the target.

I wanted to be an equipper, but I myself was ill equipped.

## SO WHAT'S THE PROBLEM?
### *When the Going Gets Tough, the Tough Send a Staff Member*

My church had the right idea when they provided opportunities for every member, even a teenager like me, to participate in the ministries of the church. The problem is, I wasn't adequately equipped for the role that I received. Equipping requires far more than placing someone in a position and asking him or her to perform a particular task! Equipping requires intentional effort to enable someone to do something that they couldn't do before so the church's capacity to fulfill the Great Commission is multiplied.

And yet, if a church member has a relative who needs to hear the gospel, who is asked to do the job? When a child has questions about how to be saved, who is the go-to person? When a youth needs discipleship and mentoring, who is expected to make time to meet weekly? If your church is typical, the answer is the pastor or some other paid staff member. You may say "every member is a minister"—but, when the going gets tough, the tough send a staff member.

What this pattern reveals practically is that, in many churches, the people haven't been equipped to do the work of ministry. The primary role of pastors and teachers is to teach truth—but teaching truth includes far more than merely imparting knowledge. Teaching truth also includes equipping God's people "for the work of ministry, for building up the body of Christ" (Ephesians 4:12).

This gap between imparting knowledge and equipping for ministry is particularly apparent in family ministry. One crucial component of a parent's "work of ministry" should be the discipleship of their children. And yet, many parents have never been equipped for this task. In a survey of churched parents with children under the age of thirteen, eighty-one percent said no church leader had ever spoken to them about how they as parents could be involved in their children's spiritual development. A separate study of student ministry values and practices revealed that, when youth ministers' efforts and expenditures were analyzed, almost nothing was being done to equip parents to engage spiritually with their teenagers. Despite placing family ministry fourth on their lists of perceived ministry priorities, youth ministers spent only three percent of their time and less than three percent of their budgets in any activity that related to the equipping of parents.[33]

"And He personally gave some to be apostles, some prophets, some evangelists, some pastors and teachers, for the training of the saints in the work of ministry, to build up the body of Christ, until we all reach unity in the faith and in the knowledge of God's Son, growing into a mature man with a stature measured by Christ's fullness. Then we will no longer be little children, tossed by the waves and blown around by every wind of teaching, by human cunning with cleverness in the techniques of deceit" (Ephesians 4:11-14).

## HOW DOES GOD'S WORD PROVIDE A NEW POSSIBILITY?
### *Learn, Practice, and Equip*

I have been a member of many churches that described themselves as "mission-minded" and "evangelistic"—but few of these churches have seen equipping parents as part of their evangelistic mission. For most parents, the closest unbelievers or young believers to them are their children. How, then, can a church expect to be effectively mission-minded or evangelistic without equipping parents to make disciples of the children in their homes?

Unfortunately, the unspoken message in many churches has been that the discipleship of children is a task best left to trained professionals. Schoolteachers are perceived as the persons responsible to grow children's minds, coaches are employed to train children's bodies, and specialized ministers at church ought to develop their souls. When it comes to schooling and coaching, such perspectives may or may not be particularly problematic. When it comes to Christian formation, however, this perspective faces an insurmountable snag: God specifically calls not only the community of faith but also the parents to engage personally in the Christian formation of children.[34]

The Christian home should be a training ground that sparks zeal for God's global mission in the world. Returning to the hand grenade metaphor, trying to develop an evangelistic church without training parents to engage their children with the gospel would be like throwing a grenade and expecting it to explode without first pulling the pin!

So how can pastors and other church leaders equip parents to disciple their children?

In the book of Ezra, the practice of God's law had lapsed among many of the Israelites (Nehemiah 8:14, 17). Ezra the scribe returned to retrain the people in God's ways and to restore worship in God's temple. According to the book that bears his name, Ezra "had set his heart to study the law of the LORD, and to do it and to teach his statutes and rules in Israel" (Ezra 7:10, ESV). Notice the pattern in Ezra's life:

> Learn ("to study the Law")
> Practice ("to do it")
> Impart and equip ("to teach")

Throughout the books of Ezra and Nehemiah, this is precisely what Ezra does. He knows God's truth, and he practices God's truth—but the scribe of Israel doesn't stop there. By the time the Israelites gather in the city square to hear the words of God, a baker's dozen of assistants stand beside Ezra, ready to train everyone who is old enough to understand (Nehemiah 8:2-8). The response of the people is renewed obedience in the form of a long-forgotten festival that involved rehearsing together God's rescue of His people from Egypt (Deuteronomy 16:13-15; Nehemiah 12:43). This festival was a family affair that reached beyond families to include orphans, widows, and immigrants (Deuteronomy 16:14). Ezra learned the truth, practiced its precepts, and then equipped others to do the same. He didn't try to teach everyone; he trained a few who taught others who then shared the great news of God's works with many more. In this, the life of Ezra the scribe points forward to One who taught with "authority, and not as their scribes" (Matthew 7:29, ESV). Jesus not only learned His Father's law, but He was also the living Word of God who perfectly fulfilled His Father's law. This living Word trained twelve and sent them out to change the world (Matthew 28:18-20).

So what does this pattern of learning, doing, and equipping have to do with family ministry today?

The order is important: Ezra learned and practiced God's ways before he tried to equip others. Church leaders who try to equip parents without discipling their own families are like a plumber who never fixes his dripping faucet or a mechanic whose dipstick is always dry.

This is not to suggest that church leaders should wait to equip their people until their own households achieve perfection! Practicing God's truth doesn't mean that you've achieved a position of perfection; practicing God's truth means moving in the same direction, seeking God's kingdom first and foremost. Even in the homes of the best leaders, diapers still get full, and gas tanks still get empty. Words are spoken that should never even have been thought, and children make choices that are far from cherubic. And yet, even with these challenges and more, every Christian household can become a context where the gospel is consistently rehearsed and where parents and children alike confess their failures to one another and learn to turn to Jesus.

A disciple-maker never outgrows being a disciple. As a disciple of Christ, you will always be learning even as you teach others to be better disciples. Only Satan the great deceiver would demand that you wait until you achieve perfection to equip others. In fact, confessing your own mistakes may encourage others to take more risks in their pursuit of God's kingdom. We learn by listening to one another's successes, but hearing about failures can teach us too.

With that in mind, here's a simple process that you might use in your church to equip parents more effectively.

# A MASTER PLAN FOR EQUIPPING PARENTS TO DISCIPLE THEIR CHILDREN

**M**

**Model What You Expect Parents to Do**

Your church's ministry to parents doesn't begin in an administrative meeting or a business session or the pastor's personal planning retreat. Equipping parents begins in the homes of the leaders in your ministry—in the pastor's den, at the deacon's dining room table, in the youth minister's car, in the bedrooms of the children of your volunteers, as they begin to develop habits of discipleship in their families. Develop a list of specific practices that will help parents to disciple their children. Begin to practice these habits in your home.

**A**

**Articulate Expected Changes with Key Leaders**

As you develop these habits in your home, help other key leaders develop habits of discipleship in their homes as well. In some churches, these key leaders may be staff members. In other churches, the key leaders may be a group of lay elders or volunteer leaders. Share with these key leaders the struggles you've faced and the victories God has given. Hold one another accountable and begin praying for specific families in your church, perhaps considering those who will struggle as well as those who are likely to develop these habits readily.

**S**

**Schedule Key Checkpoints**

Evaluate your church's schedule at two levels: (1) Has our church scheduled so many events and activities that parents may not have time to disciple their children? If so, develop a multi-year plan with clear checkpoints for merging and streamlining some ministries to provide more time for parents. (2) How can our church implement a comprehensive plan for equipping parents? What checkpoints will we put in place to evaluate our progress toward full implementation of this plan to equip parents to disciple their children?

| | |
|---|---|
| **T**<br><br>**Train Every Teacher to Be a Parent Equipper** | In a regular schedule—perhaps once every three months—gather every teacher in the church: Sunday School teachers, discipleship training teachers, adult teachers, youth teachers, children's teachers, preschool teachers. Every teacher included will lighten the load for all! Provide them with training so they become able to integrate parent-equipping into their weekly teaching. Help them to see family discipleship not as a program or an addendum to each lesson but as a lifestyle they consider as they prepare to teach each week. |
| **E**<br><br>**Empathize with Parents Who Are Struggling** | Identify specific parents who are struggling to disciple their children. Guide pastoral staff and key volunteers to meet with these parents to provide support. In some instances, it may be helpful to partner these parents with parents who are effectively discipling their children. In other instances, senior adults in your church may need to be equipped to meet with children to fill gaps where a single parent may be struggling. |
| **R**<br><br>**Recruit Families to Share Testimonies** | Identify parents who have overcome significant obstacles in the discipleship of their children. Recruit these parents to provide testimonies in worship gatherings and training meetings. Everyone expects church leaders to be able to do family ministry. Find those in non-leadership positions who are effectively discipling their children to encourage skeptics. Highlight creative approaches to discipleship to show parents how discipleship may take different forms in different households. Interview godly teenagers to find out how they might enjoy being discipled by their parents. |

## A Sample Schedule for Teacher Training Meeting

### Before the Meeting

- For a couple of weeks prior to the meeting, gather from each teacher his or her one best teaching tip or pedagogical practice.
- Select the best of these tips and practices to share in the meeting.

- Enlist—from within your church or perhaps from a denominational agency—expert practitioners in teaching each broad age grouping (for example: preschoolers, children, youth and young adults, middle adults, and senior adults).
- Consider a drawing so teachers win door prizes that will help them teach more effectively.

### During the Meeting

- Begin with a top-ten list of the best teaching tips from your teachers (10 minutes).
- Send teachers into breakout sessions with expert practitioners to sharpen their teaching skills (25 minutes).
- Gather teachers around tables of five-to-ten persons each, organized according to the age group they teach. Guide the discussions at the tables to focus on the question: How can I integrate parent-equipping into my weekly teaching? For teachers of preschoolers, this might result in a plan to place a family devotional guide in each parents hands as she or he picks up their child, perhaps with a simple encouragement that you would be glad to meet with parents to talk about how to use this guide. Senior adult Sunday School teachers might focus on how to share their wisdom—both their successes and failures in family discipleship—with specific parents in the church. Youth mentors might work on ways to provide parents with weekly discussion questions that spark discussions between parents and children that apply each week's teaching at church (15-20 minutes).
- Close the training by gathering and sharing the best ideas from the roundtable discussions. Draw names for door prizes (5-10 minutes).

*After the Meeting*

- Follow up with teachers, asking how they have implemented the changes that were discussed in the meeting. Find out what challenges they are facing.
- Use the successes and challenges you hear from teachers as a basis for planning your next teacher training.

## YOU ARE INADEQUATE—AND THAT'S GOOD NEWS

While it may seem discouraging at first, the great news is that you are inadequate for the task of equipping parents to disciple their children. That is why God sent His Son to redeem us and His Spirit to reside within us. As you move your ministry to emphasize the equipping of parents, remember that the same Spirit who is transforming you is also present in the life of every other believer. Trust the power of God's Spirit and the proclamation of God's Word to bring transformation. Don't focus on parent-equipping; center your life and ministry on the Master Equipper, the Holy Spirit.

The goal is not merely to place people in positions—that's what happened to me when I hurled that hand grenade of a sermon so many years ago. The goal is to equip the people of God so the Spirit of God can work through them to the glory of God. What that requires from us is to learn God's truth, to do what it says, and to multiply the impact of God's truth by equipping others to do the same, beginning in their homes.

# CHAPTER SEVEN

# BE A FAMILY FOR EMERGING ADULTS

*John David Trentham*

n college, I watched as Ted joined the ranks of the "de-churched." Similar to the droves of others like him, he did not leave with a chip on his shoulder or because of a revolutionary shift in his system of beliefs. His drift away from the body of Christ was not premeditated. Through his teenage years, Ted connected closely with his home church. His primary circle of friends was in the youth group; he was part of almost every major activity and retreat; and he participated in most small group fellowship and discipleship functions. When he moved away to college, he simply lost touch with his nucleus of thriving relationships. At the same time, he established personal connections in his new, secular context at a rapid pace. Meanwhile, there was no one in his home church who was prepared to retain a connection with him.

Ted's story is unfortunately indicative of a representative mass of young adults. There are, however, those who deepen their relationship with Christ as they move through the college and young adult experience. In such cases, the local church is the linchpin in the process of discipleship. For example, consider the case of Adrian, through whom I, as her young adult pastor, witnessed the effectiveness of biblical discipleship with young adults.

As a typical emerging adult, Adrian attends college, works full-time, and maintains bonds of friendship and acquaintances through numerous social outlets, all while remaining closely involved in the life of her family. The first time I remember speaking to her was at a gathering of young adults who were collaborating to accumulate resources to contribute to a humanitarian aid ministry. Her interest in collaborative responsibility and service would prove to be more than a one-time decision to participate in a project promoting the welfare of others; it would also be an inroad to pursuing the course of discipleship within the family of God.

Earlier in life, Adrian had made the decision to become a Christian, but had not been baptized and had never applied her faith as a relevant part of her life. Her noninvolvement in the church was about to shift dramatically, due in no small part to the fact that one of her first experiences with the young adults at our church was in the context of serving the needs of others in Jesus' name. She would come to associate her faith with more than a personal set of beliefs or morals, but rather with an interdependent commitment to Godly obedience.

Adrian continued to participate in various small-group and church-wide service and outreach efforts. Then, she also became a faithful attender of our worship services and the young adults' small group Bible study. This group delved deeply into Scripture, progressing deliberately through entire books of the Bible with the intention of understanding the original message, and maturing through lifestyle application. Over time, Adrian advanced from simply observing to more relational interaction. She realized that Scripture is relevant to everyday life and that genuine discussion about the Bible among fellow believers offers the benefits of understanding the Word more clearly and the simultaneous opportunity of helping others to understand.

Through her involvement with a young ladies' discipleship group, she formed a special bond with my wife. This relationship provided the open forum to talk about issues that were purely practical, concerns that were intensely personal, and topics that were deeply spiritual. Adrian came to realize the importance of having a trusted spiritual advisor who cared about her and could identify with her. In this context, when the issue of baptism was discussed, Adrian was initially apprehensive. In time, however, she decided based on her own conviction that she must be faithful and obedient.

Adrian's first step of obedience was actually the culmination of a journey that had begun a couple of years earlier. As she stood in the baptismal water in front of her church family, the pastor asked, "Adrian, who is Lord of your life?" When she unashamedly proclaimed the name of Jesus, she did so as a devoted disciple.

## SO WHAT'S THE PROBLEM?

### The Church's Struggle to Engage Effectively With Emerging Adults

So are emerging adults impressionable young people, or are they responsible adults?

The answer is, "Yes."

Today, it is common for individuals to spend up to ten years between high school graduation and marriage, taking their time to experience the new lifestyle of early adulthood with all its many new freedoms before really growing up and settling down. This stage of life has become known as "emerging adulthood, a period of development between adolescence and young adulthood in which young people are no longer adolescents but have not yet attained full adult status.[35] Even though emerging adulthood is a distinct phase of life, it is in many ways a state of limbo, separate from both teenage adolescence and full-scale adulthood, but including a mixture of both. The overarching goal throughout emerging adulthood is to "stand on one's own two feet"—to become independent. This is a very important consideration in reaching out to emerging adults. They do not necessarily want to abandon their values and the faith of their upbringing, but they do want to put distance between their beliefs and the faith-assumptions of their parents. They prefer to base their beliefs and values on their own personally-vetted convictions rather than their parents' inherited views. With that in mind, ministries to emerging adults must equip, but not indoctrinate, individuals with the tools by which to personally analyze the legitimacy of their worldview and practice.

Any discussion of ministries to emerging adults must take into consideration the fact that local churches are struggling to reach them. Most church dropouts leave the church between the ages of eighteen and twenty-two—like Ted—and the church is the only institution that emerging adults leave in mass. Contrary to what some may assume, however, even unchurched emerging adults are generally open to dialogue about the Christian faith, and they are willing to study the Bible with a friend.[36] Almost half of personally invited, unchurched emerging adults are open to attending a small group with a friend. Like Adrian, they are not closed off.

### KEY TRUTH

"Let no one despise your youth; instead, you should be an example to the believers in speech, in conduct, in love, in faith, in purity" (1 Timothy 4:12).

While there is much to be said for modes and methods of parental involvement in the spiritual lives of emerging adults, the intent of the remainder of this chapter is to offer some guiding principles and applications for how the church must engage emerging adults in the process of discipleship, through the lens of a family-equipping approach. Just as parents of children and youth must not surrender their discipling responsibilities to trained professionals, so the faith-family must collectively resolve neither to abrogate nor delegate their responsibility to incorporate and disciple emerging adults.

## HOW DOES GOD'S WORD PROVIDE A NEW POSSIBILITY?
### *Church-as-Family for Emerging Adults*

The biblical identification of the Christian community is distinguished in terms of being a family with God as Father. Thus, Jesus taught His followers to address God as "our Father" (Matthew 6:9). The apostle Paul refers to the church as "God's household, which is the church of the living God, the pillar and foundation of the truth" (1 Timothy 3:15). The relationship enjoyed by all believers in the church is that of God's adopted children (see Romans 8:15, 23; Galatians 4:5; Ephesians 1:5)—a status that is made possible only through the redemptive work of God's only begotten Son (Galatians 4:1-7). All believers share a sibling relationship as children of God and recipients of the Father's unconditional love (1 John 3:1).

Understanding the concept of the church as a family is essential to the discipleship efforts of any group within the church, particularly emerging adults. "Family ministry" is a term that is associated with ministries of the church that are geared toward children and youth, with particular emphasis given to the primary role of parents in the process of their children's spiritual formation. Discussions of family ministry generally address only school-age children and youth along with their parents, but it is necessary to demonstrate that in the context of emerging adult discipleship, family ministry is a priority of the church too. Church leaders must realize the tendency when promoting family ministry to unintentionally downplay the status of adults who are single. Dick Purnell puts it this way, "Now I am all for a family church, but as far as I can see, it is the family of God church, not the family of married people church." He continues:

> A church near my home placed a huge sign on the front lawn: "This is the Year of the Family." I tried to tell the pastor that the hidden message was "Singles unwanted for twelve months." Announcements are enthusiastically presented in the church service: "We are going

to have our annual family gathering. Bring your whole family." The singles look at each other and say, "I guess they don't want us."[37]

A focus on equipping families should be the outflow of a healthy church family that seamlessly integrates each unique member with the same spirit of adoption in Christ (Romans 8:15). It is this familial identity as adopted children of God that provides the foundational unity of every local church in which discipleship takes place. Ministry to emerging adults must focus on discipling men and women in the light of God's calling for most of them to become godly marriage partners and parents. It is also important, however, to disciple them in light of their present life-state of singleness. Emerging adulthood is not merely a holding cell for individuals until they get married. Emerging adulthood is a stage of great opportunity: to live constantly in recognition of one's adopted status in Christ, to ground one's gender identity in God's design, and to pursue relationships as biblical men and women who understand the primacy of devoting one's entire life, including one's relationships, to the glory of God for all eternity.

## IDEAS FOR MERGING EMERGING ADULTS INTO YOUR CHURCH FAMILY[38]

| PRIORITY | FOUNDATION | APPLICATION |
|---|---|---|
| 1. Establish and Preserve Community | Emerging adults seek authentic community. Such authenticity is felt through ongoing, relational connections—not conjured by the occasional email message or special big event. Be purposeful in creating community among your emerging adults. | Consider replacing the holiday-break mega-conference with a community-discipleship retreat that promotes relationship development through meaningful interaction that is casual and personal. |

| PRIORITY | FOUNDATION | APPLICATION |
|---|---|---|
| 2. Generate Intergenerational Connections | The notion that emerging adults are disinterested in maintaining or building relationships with older, more experienced adults is a myth. Even while they are learning to stand on their own two feet, the lives and witness of parents continue to influence religious convictions in emerging adults—more so, in fact, than teenage friends or peers. Also, non-parental influencers within local churches who serve as personal mentors have an enduring impact on the spiritual lives of young adults. | Many churches have programs, sometimes called "Barnabas Ministries" that connect members of the church to college students during the academic semesters. The idea is simply to enlist members, families, or small groups within your church to offer frequent tokens of encouragement to students while they are taking classes. Senior adults are particularly interested in this ministry. Encouragement can come in the form of prayer notes, encouraging emails, and care packages or gift cards for coffee during midterm and finals weeks. |
| 3. Hold Them Responsible | For emerging adults, a great deal of credibility hangs on the church's action toward those in difficult circumstances. Challenge your emerging adults to make sacrificial commitments to serve in ministries that provide for those with physical and emotional needs. | Rather than a "leadership team" of all-star young adult Christians, begin a "service team" that is open to anyone willing to serve who is also committed to pursuing biblical standards for spiritual devotion and uprightness. Doing so genuinely encourages the essence of gospel-centered service: merciful, compassionate outreach that is primarily intent on responsibly engaging people as individuals rather than potential converts. It allows you to set high expectations for all those who take part in ministry, not just a select few. |

| PRIORITY | FOUNDATION | APPLICATION |
|---|---|---|
| 4. Engage those Away from Home | One of the obvious contributing factors to the dropout of emerging adults from church after they graduate high school is the disconnect when students move away to colleges and universities. This not only affects those students who are away but also those who stay at home. Think of it this way: Suppose you have ten high school graduates in your church who have been faithfully involved in student ministry. These students have formed bonds not only with the church family but also with each other, through small group discipleship, retreats, mission trips, and social interactions. If five of those students leave town permanently, the group changes dramatically and there is a tendency on the part of those who stay home to retreat from the church. Two crucial steps must be taken:

1. Ensure that

*Continued on next page* | Here are a couple of specific ways to engage those away from home:

(a) Virtual community. For students who are away at school, create an online blog-network of students who participate in an ongoing, discipleship discussion group. The basic idea is that on-campus students have a blog site through which they can freely discuss any issue related to their campus experience, share prayer requests, and maintain a close, family connection with each other while they are away at school. New threads for various topics of discussion can be created, and over time, as more entries are made, an incredible collaborative resource emerges. This could easily be organized using a book such as Jonathan Morrow's *Welcome to College*. As students work through chapters together, encourage them to respond and interact by posting their thoughts, reactions, and experiences on the blog site. When these students come back home for visits and holidays, they are thus more likely to treasure the opportunity to be with their church family in person.

(b) Visitation. Make it a priority to visit college students who are away from home one time each academic semester. Depending on the size of your church and number of students you have, there may be several who attend various schools that are too far away for a daytime trip there and back. You will need to do very little arm-twisting to get your young adults to visit their friends who live away from home. During these campus visits,

*Continued on next page* |

| PRIORITY | FOUNDATION | APPLICATION |
|---|---|---|
| 4. Engage those Away from Home (Cont.) | connections are formed between your emerging adults and senior high school students before they graduate.<br><br>2. Do everything in your power to build lines of communication and discipleship connection between your ministry leaders, on-campus students, and emerging adults at home. | a powerful message of genuine concern and care is communicated to your on-campus students—who will be deeply appreciative. Campus-bound students realize, "Wow, my friends and church leaders are not only thinking about me and praying for me, but they are taking the time to travel to where I am and meet me on my own turf, to experience my new life and context." Do you have students attending schools with strong athletic programs? If so, you likely also have already-organized delegations of campus connection groups! Particularly with football and basketball games, the experience of an athletic event is often an all-day affair, and your church members who attend are probably going with their family or friends. This could be as simple as meeting up in the concourse of the arena at halftime, buying the student a hot dog, and asking any prayer concerns the student may have. |

## Discipling Those Who Are In-Between

The core values of family ministry apply directly to the discipleship of emerging adults—but in a different way than in other age-graded ministries. Family ministry to children and teens entails equipping parents to disciple their children diligently. The responsibility of discipling individuals who are somewhere in between the modes of parental dependence and independence requires its own unique emphases and sensitivities. If emerging adults are relationally engaged and made an essential part of the community of faith, however, they will serve the kingdom alongside their brothers and sisters, and they will mature in Christlikeness.

# CHAPTER EIGHT

# BE A FAMILY FOR BLENDED FAMILIES

*Joshua A. Remy*

L ike so many couples before them, Mike and Joanne scheduled some time with their pastor to talk through their recent marriage difficulties. The pastor, who had performed their wedding ceremony, agreed to see them and help them work through their struggles. He met with Mike first and sifted through a multitude of issues that had come up in their four-year marriage. Mike seemed like he wanted to give up, but his pastor urged him to keep trying. Mike agreed but he still believed the problems were too many to overcome. The meeting with Joanne didn't go much better. She saw many of the same issues in their marriage, but had a slightly sunnier attitude. She believed with all of her heart that they could work through these differences.

After hearing their separate sides of the story, their pastor brought them together again in hopes that the real problems would surface. They absolutely did. On their own, Mike and Joanne had talked about the common marital problems of unresolved conflict and poor communication and cited many different examples, but when they were together, one consistent issue came up: parenting.

Mike and Joanne had only been married four years, but each had a daughter from a previous marriage. Mike's daughter was a teenager, and Joanne had a daughter just starting school. Each one had sole custody, and they clearly loved their children. The problem was that they practiced very different parenting styles. On some issues, Mike was permissive while Joanne was rigid. At other times, Joanne was the soft one and Mike held firm. When push came to shove, each one sided with their own daughters rather than with each other. They couldn't seem to get on the same page, and this division was threatening to destroy their marriage.

The pastor reminded them about their discussions in premarital counseling, but the couple pointed out that—even with this preparation—they never expected the magnitude of their current struggles. Each of them had a pre-established relationship that they brought into the marriage; right now, these relationships with their children seemed stronger than the marriage itself. They had a "perforated" marriage of sorts, ready to be ripped apart with minimal mess. If they so chose, each one could step away from their relationship with their own child. The difficulty for the pastor was that their entire marital struggle seemed to stem from differences in parenting—all this, despite many discussions during counseling and deep involvement in the church.

All marriages suffer challenges caused by parenting, but many blended families struggle not to put their previous family relationships before their current marriage covenant. In addition to the stress of a new marriage, spouses in blended families have the pressures of learning the personalities, likes, and dislikes of their spouse's children. Some say it feels like birthing multiple children at once! How can the church help couples like Mike and Joanne to develop marriages that reflect the true purpose of marriage—to stand as a living image of the exquisite intimacy that Jesus Christ enjoys with His church? (Ephesians 5:22-33).

## SO WHAT'S THE PROBLEM?

## Why Your Church Can't Hide From Broken and Blended Families

The United States government no longer gathers certain statistics on marital status and family structures. However, even in the 1990s, it was predicted that the number of blended and single-parent families in the United States would outpace traditional families in the opening decades of the twenty-first century.[39] It's tempting to pretend that divorce and remarriage don't happen—but, for churches that yearn to see the gospel bring new life to broken people, that's not an option. Divorce is never God's design, but it happens, sometimes for reasons that are right and sometimes for reasons that are wrong. Effective family ministry acknowledges the realities of divorce and remarriage while refusing to compromise the ideal that God has revealed in His written Word.

## What Does the Bible Teach About Divorce and Remarriage?[40]

1. Divorce distorts God's ideal (Matthew 19:4-6).
2. Divorce destroys a relationship that God designed to depict the gospel (Ephesians 5:18-23).
3. God despises divorce (Malachi 2:14-16).
4. God allowed divorce for the purpose of protecting the innocent (Deuteronomy 24:1-4).
5. God forbids divorce except when one partner is sexually unfaithful or when one partner abandons the other (Matthew 5:32; 19:8-9; 1 Corinthians 7:12-40).
6. Since divorce is allowed in cases of sexual unfaithfulness or abandonment, the believer "is not bound" in the aftermath of such a divorce—that is to say, he or she is free to marry another believer (1 Corinthians 7:15).
7. The grace and power of God are available to pardon your past divorce and to prevent your future divorce.

## HOW DOES GOD'S WORD PROVIDE A NEW POSSIBILITY?

### *Biblical Foundations for Ministry With Single Parents and Blended Families*

The Bible is filled with broken and blended families. Abraham conceived a son with Hagar while waiting for God to give him a son through Sarah; the result was family conflict that continues to this very day (Genesis 16:12). Abraham's great grandchildren had one father, but four different mothers (Genesis 29:16–30:12). The prophet Samuel was born to a family with conflicts that drove his mother to tears (1 Samuel 1:1-20). And don't forget kings like David and Solomon who multiplied wives despite God's command for kings to refrain from this practice (Deuteronomy 17:17; 1 Samuel 18:18-27; 1 Kings 11:3). Then there was the widow at Zarephath—a single mother who served Elijah even as she struggled to make ends meet (1 Kings 17). You might even say that Jesus' family was a blended household, since Joseph was not Jesus' biological father.

Much ink has been spilled over whether and when Scripture permits divorce and remarriage—and these are important issues. Yet too little attention has typically been given to how churches can serve families affected by divorce and remarriage. One result is that Christians may be uncomfortable and uncertain about how to deal with divorce. As Gretchen Goldsmith recently pointed out,

> Of all of the industrialized countries, the United States is at the top for divorce rates. Nearly one-third of American adults who've ever married have been divorced at least once. This is not a new trend. America's high divorce rate has astounded observers for more than two hundred years.
>
> No matter how strongly we feel about the importance of faithful marriages, church pews are filled with people who've gone through the breakdown of a marriage, whether they discuss it publicly or not. For some people it may be a secret that not even the pastor knows. In fact, the embarrassment and awkwardness causes many people who are separated or going through a divorce to drop out of the church

and take their children with them. They find it hard to face others, and many never return.[41]

The focus of this chapter is how best to minister to broken and blended families. With that in mind, let's look at four foundations for ministry to nontraditional families.

**The church is called to serve every family regardless of their origin:** Some families may be broken and blended due to tragedies that no one could have avoided. Others may have been formed as a result of sinful choices by unbelievers, or even by believers—but the people of God are called to love them regardless of their origins. Serving families formed due to sinful choices doesn't mean that we're placing God's stamp of approval on those choices! It simply means we value them as people formed in God's image who need the healing only the gospel can bring, just like us. The woman Jesus met in Samaria had a household that was about as broken, blended, and non-traditional as you can get! (John 4:16-26). Yet Jesus honored her and shared the gospel with her. As a result, she became a missionary to the people of Samaria (John 4:27-42). Christian care does not contradict confronting people with their sin; instead, Christian love and care create a context where we can be corrected without being crushed. Even in the most battered and shattered families, there are fragments of the design that God the Father wove into His creation in the very beginning (Ephesians 3:14-15).

**The church is called to care for the needs of the vulnerable:** Whether due to death, divorce, sinful choices, or some combination of factors, nearly every blended family or single-parent home has been scarred by crisis. Throughout the Scriptures, the people of God are called to care for those that are vulnerable, particularly the fatherless and widows (Exodus 22:22; Deuteronomy 14:29; Isaiah 1:17; 1 Timothy 5:7-14; James 1:27). Sometimes, this support is material and financial (2 Corinthians 9:11; Ephesians 4:28; 1 Timothy 6:18). Other times, we care for one another by sharing spiritual and emotional burdens (Romans 12:10; 1 Corinthians 12:25; Galatians 6:2). It may take a child or an ex-spouse years to unravel the grieving processes that grow out of the crises caused by divorce or the death of a spouse. The church is called to step into the lives of hurting people and to become a means by which the gospel brings healing and transformation.

**The church is a community both of holiness and of diversity:** A church that reaches its community will be a church filled with blended families and less-than-pristine backgrounds. "No sexually immoral people, idolaters, adulterers, or anyone practicing homosexuality, no thieves, greedy people, drunkards, verbally abusive people, or swindlers will inherit God's kingdom," Paul wrote to the Corinthians; then, he added these words: "And some of you used to be like this" (1 Corinthians 6:9-11). The Corinthian church was filled with people whose pasts were distorted by sin. Not only that, but there were also moral failures in some of their lives even after they became believers (1 Corinthians 5:1-5). Simply put, the families in the Corinthian church were far from traditional households in the modern sense of the term! When addressing the Corinthians, Paul refused to compromise God's design for the people of God. Yet he also called the church to extend communion and comfort when errant members turned from their sin (2 Corinthians 2:5-11).

# PRIORITIES, PLANS, AND PRACTICES FOR SERVING SINGLE PARENTS AND BLENDED FAMILIES

| PRIORITY | PLAN | PRACTICE |
|----------|------|----------|
| **1. Support** | | |
| • In addition to the stress of a new marriage, parents in blended families may be learning the personalities, likes, and dislikes of their spouse's children. Some report that this feels like birthing multiple children at once! Both spouses may be struggling with guilt over their failed marriage or renewed grief over the death of their previous spouse. At least one of the families will be experiencing the stress of moving into a new house. | • Do you know how many single parents live in your neighborhood? | • Using a website such as www.zip-codes.com, you can find out the percentage of single mothers and fathers who live in your church's ZIP code. If the percentage of single parents in your church is radically lower than the percentage in your neighborhood, make outreach to single-parent families a consistent prayer focus. |
| • A single parent feels many of the same pressures as a blended family—but without a mate with whom to share the stresses. Their income may be their family's only means of support, adding additional stress. | • Has your church asked single parents about their primary needs? If not, it is possible that you are offering programs to address problems that these parents aren't actually facing. | • Create an anonymous online survey to gather information about the needs of single parents and blended families in your congregation. Provide the link in a church newsletter or other similar resource that goes out to the entire church. |
| • After divorce, children frequently experience humiliation, guilt, and distrust. | • Has your church asked parents in blended families about their primary needs? If not, it is possible that you are offering programs to address problems that these parents aren't actually facing. | • Based on the data you collect from your survey, develop one specific support system for single parents or blended families that did not exist previously in your church. |

| PRIORITY | PLAN | PRACTICE |
|---|---|---|

## 2. Integration

**PRIORITY**

- Many congregations, with the best of intentions, group all singles together—but this practice secludes many single parents from needed interactions with other parents and families.

- In some instances, congregations are uncertain how to respond to single parents and blended families; the result is these individuals are excluded from service and fellowship.

- If an individual's sinful choices contributed to divorce or to single parenthood, the church should make clear provisions for confession, repentance, and renewed welcome into communion. Simply because someone divorces does not mean that person is sinning; it may be that they are the innocent partner and their spouse has sinned against them. Churches tend to err in one of two directions, neither of which is biblical: (1) Never asking difficult questions or dealing with the situation at all—which may result in a lack of support for an innocent partner or in allowing someone to serve who

*Continued on next page*

**PLAN**

- If a single parent visits your church and asks, "Which small group should I attend?" where do you send them? Have these groupings been strategically selected, or are they based on convenience or incorrect assumptions?

- Does your congregation have a clear understanding of your church's practices and processes of church discipline?

- Does your congregation have a clear understanding of what Scripture teaches about divorce? If not, church members may be uncertain how to respond to divorced persons. The result may be unintended exclusion of blended and single-parent families.

**PRACTICE**

- Carefully consider how your church groups single parents. In many congregations, single parents may be best served in a multigenerational group from a variety of life stages.

- Teach a series on biblical church discipline that articulates the specific ways your congregation calls people to repentance.

- Teach a series on marriage, divorce, and remarriage that graciously articulates requirements and possibilities for divorced persons and single parents to serve in the church.

| PRIORITY | PLAN | PRACTICE |
|---|---|---|
| is engaged in unrepentant sin. (2) Shunning or excluding an individual who is involved in a divorce—which may result in a lack of support for an innocent partner or in a failure to call a sinning member to repentance. | | |

**3. Preparation**

| PRIORITY | PLAN | PRACTICE |
|---|---|---|
| • The church should be prepared to provide divorced persons and single parents with gospel-centered equipping for their future—whether long-term singleness or remarriage.<br><br>• If a man and woman desire to marry and one or both of them were previously married, the church should be prepared to equip them for the unique challenges faced by blended families.<br><br>• If a divorced person or single parent is or becomes a Christian, he or she has a place in God's plan and a future among God's people. Churches should provide clear vision and direction for these individuals to serve. | • Does your congregation provide counseling or small-group ministries to help divorced persons work through their grief, prepare for a new future, and seek God-centered healing of unhealthy relational patterns?<br><br>• Does your congregation have a clear premarital counseling curriculum in place for persons who have been previously married?<br><br>• Does your church have a clear plan for finding appropriate places of service for every Christian? | • Train every small-group leader to counsel and to care for divorced persons.<br><br>• Develop or locate premarital counseling curriculum for previously married persons. Include in this curriculum several post-wedding check-ups. Particularly for previously married persons, many of the most difficult stresses emerge in the months after the wedding.<br><br>• Develop guidelines with key volunteer coordinators so every faithful believer—regardless of their background—has a place to serve in your congregation. |

## What Will You Do?

Right now, the future of Mike and Joanne's marriage remains up in the air. Their pastor is continuing to work and pray with them, but they need more than the pastor alone. They need their church family to stand alongside them and to fight for the future of their marriage. Chances are, there are single parents and blended families much like Mike and Joanne in your church too. Just like Mike and Joanne, they need their church family to stand with them and to support them. Will you?

## CHAPTER NINE

# BE A FAMILY BY GIVING GRANDPARENTS A VISION FOR THE GENERATIONS

*Gary May*

I t was 10:00 a.m., and I stopped at a convenience store with my oldest son, his wife, and my newborn granddaughter. We were on our way to spend a couple of days with my mother. When my son came out of the store, he was sporting a burrito fresh from under the warmer lights. The sight of him emerging from the convenience store, burrito in hand, took me back some fifteen years earlier. Back then, his grandfather would take him to a convenience store that was part of the same chain each Sunday night after church. As my son piled back into the car, we reminisced about Pa Pa, the joyful moments we had shared, and the influence he had on his grandchildren.

The joy of attending a church that my two sons enjoyed with their grandparents is almost indescribable. When they visited their other set of grandparents, they discovered the same values. In both homes, the Scripture was opened and read at the family gathering for Christmas. Bibles were commonplace in multiple rooms in each of their grandparent's homes. When each of these boys came under conviction of the Holy Spirit and turned to Jesus, both sets of grandparents celebrated their salvation. I am unspeakably thankful for a family where we witness multigenerational faith in Jesus Christ.

## SO WHAT'S THE PROBLEM?
### *A Daunting but Necessary Task*

Even as I rejoice in the multigenerational faithfulness that my sons have seen, I know that this is not everyone's experience. Due to divorce, many children have more than two sets of grandparents with radically different values from one another. The number of single parents has rapidly increased in the past few decades, resulting in expanded roles for many grandparents.[42] The escalation of families with incarcerated parents has produced more and more children who are being raised by their grandparents.

So what do these patterns mean for the day-by-day ministries of the local church?

Simply this: Any church that is serious about equipping families to disciple the next generation must equip not only parents but also grandparents.

## HOW DOES GOD'S WORD PROVIDE A NEW POSSIBILITY?
### *The Power of a Faithful Grandparent*

Late in his life, Paul the apostle called on Timothy to continue the mission the apostles began. Writing from a Roman prison, Paul pointed to the faith of Timothy's mother and grandmother as a heritage that had provided a template for Timothy's faith. Paul seems to have been well acquainted with these two dear saints since he spoke so warmly and personally about their sincere faith.

Timothy was a fortunate young man! He had a mother and a grandmother who were so faithful that the apostle Paul applauded their sincerity. Timothy

"I thank God, whom I serve with a clear conscience as my ancestors did, when I constantly remember you in my prayers night and day. Remembering your tears, I long to see you so that I may be filled with joy, clearly recalling your sincere faith that first lived in your grandmother Lois, then in your mother Eunice, and that I am convinced is in you also" (2 Timothy 1:3-5).

was also fortunate because his mother and grandmother seem to have taught him God's Word. Timothy's father was a Greek while his mother was Jewish, yet Timothy had known the Scriptures since his childhood (2 Timothy 3:15). Paul credits this biblical knowledge to Timothy's grandmother and mother. Whether it is allegiance to a particular sports team or commitments to be avid hunters, family traditions are a powerful shaping force in our lives.[43] Paul points to the family pattern of faithfulness to Scripture to encourage this young leader in the early New Testament church.

When parents are focused on raising children as disciples of Christ, grandparents are in a unique position to partner with them by being godly examples and by teaching the same truths. This is not an area of life where grandparents should be passive! By having consistent conversations with the parents and the children, grandparents can become familiar with issues with which their grandchildren are dealing at different stages in their lives. When a child is learning his or her ABC's or 123's, it is natural for grandparents to join in the training. Grandparents may purchase books for their grandchildren, sit them on their knees and coach them, perhaps even sing songs to encourage them. How much greater if grandparents will practice the same patterns in the spiritual realm!

Just like grandparents coach grandchildren in the basics of math or the mechanics of baseball, they can encourage them to learn biblical facts and applications to life. Does your church provide resources to assist grandparents? Do you encourage them to join in the spiritual formation of their grandchildren? Do you use time in their small groups to reinforce their responsibility to guide their grandchildren in the ways of Christ?

But, of course, not all parents are seeking to raise their children as disciples of Christ. In such circumstances, the influence of a godly grandparent is even more crucial. Again, a primary means of passing down the heritage of living for Jesus is just that, a life lived for Jesus. But example alone will not suffice. Jesus was an example but he didn't stop at being an example; he also spoke God's words as well (Matthew 4:23). Through their words, grandparents can teach, they can bless, or they can curse (James 3:10). Grandparents are in a unique relationship with children which allows them to be very effective with words of blessing, teaching, and grace.

## Maximizing the Investments of Grandparents

With that in mind, let's look at three specific ways that churches can maximize grandparents' capacity to invest in their children's lives.

1. **Partner with grandparents in the discipleship of their grandchildren by providing reliable resources:** Grandparents are commonly found browsing the children's department in bookstores—both Christian and non-Christian—as well as church libraries. Usually, they're seeking gifts or resources to help them to connect with grandchildren who are coming for a visit. How can your congregation equip grandparents with doctrinally sound, age-appropriate resources? Perhaps you could provide a list of books, grouped according to age and stage of life. Maybe the church librarian could create a display of devotional guides for families. However you choose to present the resources, enable grandparents to take their grandchildren with them to the church library or Christian bookstore to select a resource to read, watch, or listen to together.[45]

2. *Provide opportunities for grandparents to encourage one another and to share ideas.* By the time most believers reach the stage in life to be grandparents, they should be fairly mature in feeding themselves from the Scripture. If they intend to influence their grandchildren's lives with the truths of God, they must possess knowledge of the truth. But God did not call us to serve in a vacuum. Instead, God gave us the gift of the church.

Grandparents are sometimes greatly discouraged because their children are not raising the next generation to love Jesus. The church can reach out to grandparents in two specific ways: First, the leaders in the children's department can be especially sensitive to different grandparents' circumstances. Pray for grandparents who are struggling to disciple grandchildren whose parents aren't believers. Children's workers and church leadership can make it a point to talk with grandparents in order to discern specific needs and to gain understanding of their unique situations. Second, gather grandparents together from time to time, with a specific agenda for encouraging one another and sharing ideas.

3. *Look for opportunities to recognize and to affirm grandparents who bring their grandchildren to church.* Grandparents who bring their grandchildren to church need to find a welcoming environment. They are sometimes self-conscious because of circumstances that have required them to serve as the primary spiritual guides in their grandchildren's lives. Relieve this self-consciousness by affirming and celebrating their efforts.

In my own context, the situations of grandparents in relationship to their grandchildren are especially diverse. Included in our fellowship are grandparents whose children and grandchildren attend church with them, alongside grandparents who have grandchildren living in their household without their parents. Several grandparents bring their grandchildren to multiple activities connected with the church even though the parents of the children do not attend. There are also grandparents who have grandchildren with special needs. In addition, there are grandparents who are serving in both the grandparent and parental roles.

Grandparents who are raising grandchildren may feel trapped at times. Their financial resources are sometimes stretched very thin. They need a supporting environment filled with Christ-like love and acceptance. Involving these grandparents in some of the children's ministries helps the children see their grandparents actively serving in Christ's church.

So how can your church turn these principles into practical patterns of ministry?

| CHURCH MINISTRY EMPHASIS | INVESTMENT OPPORTUNITIES FOR GRANDPARENTS |
|---|---|
| 1. Develop Discipleship Resources with Grandparents in Mind | Many churches already provide resources on a weekly basis that could provide great guidance to grandparents as they seek to use their influence to lead their grandchildren to walk with Christ. If the grandparents attend the same church as the children, the task is fairly simple. Teachers in the children's department are overjoyed to have a grandparent ask them what the children are studying in any particular week. Often they have take-home resources relating to the weekly lesson. Many church programs include those that challenge the children to learn memory verses each week. This can be a natural connection between children, grandparents, and church. Grandparents and children do not even have to live in the same community. Also, the outline from the pastor's weekly messages serves as a great resource to equip grandparents to talk about faith issues with their grandchildren. Many churches provide a take-home discussion guide designed specifically to facilitate spiritual dialogue among families. Grandparents who do not attend the same church as their grandchildren can make a simple phone or email request for these materials. |

**2. Cultivate Patterns of Fellowship and Spiritual Encouragement for Grandparents**

One grandmother I know established a one-week summer retreat, lovingly entitled "Grammy Camp," just to connect and invest in the lives of her grandchildren. She let all of her children know well in advance that she would be expecting all of her grandchildren to stay with her through that week. She enlisted the help of her own mother and her sister to plan the week and help transport the kids. The camp is always full of fun activities helping this grandmother cultivate a relationship with her grandchildren. She takes the opportunity to share truths from God's Word at the same time. Because this grandmother is a faithful follower of Christ, her influence as a godly example is multiplied. The practice is contagious. Other grandparents are continually asking this faithful grandmother for ideas on how to plan such a week for their own grandkids. Some churches are developing family camps where the church body and many families of the church body conduct a camp together. When the church plans family outings together, such as family camp, special emphases placed on including the grandparents in the activity prove to be spiritually beneficial.

Encouragement during times of difficulty is equally important. Grandparents are dealing with so many issues in the lives of their children and grandchildren; they sometimes find themselves short on wisdom for the circumstance at hand. It is through fellowship in a local congregation that grandparents can share tears of joy and pain when it comes to ministering to their grandchildren.

| CHURCH MINISTRY EMPHASIS | INVESTMENT OPPORTUNITIES FOR GRANDPARENTS |
|---|---|
| **3. Create Opportunities for Grandparents to Serve and Celebrate their Service** | The most sensitive person in the congregation to the opportunities presented by special-needs children is often that of a grandmother. She realizes the necessity of special ministries for mothers of special needs children and the need for a safe, secure environment for their grandchildren. The worker-to-child ratio for these ministries is especially high and can be a great place for grandparents to connect their faith, home, and church. Also, the environment of worship is essential for the grandparent as well as the grandchildren. Through the many ministries of the church, grandparents have the privilege of watching their grandchildren interact with other believing children while learning the precious truths of God's Word in many venues. Through ministries such as children's choirs, drama, Bible drills, Vacation Bible Schools, camps, and retreats, children find many opportunities with an intentional environment of worship. When grandparents lend their assistance to these ministries, a shared experience provides an even greater opportunity for shared faith that transcends generations. |

# GRAY-HAIRED CROWN OF GLORY

One of the primary goals in our practices of ministry should be to engender multigenerational faithfulness so that all generations walk together with God. The testimony of the Old and New Testaments reveals God's plan for a community of faith where His people live in harmony and fellowship with one another. Grandparents are in a unique position to influence a new generation of disciples of Jesus Christ. Although my dad passed away over a decade ago, the time he invested spiritually in the lives of his grandchildren continues to produce a harvest. Several of his grandchildren are actively serving in churches. They are committed to passing down the legacy of a strong Christian faith to his great-grandchildren and his great-great-grandchildren. One grandson, active in his local church, periodically is given the opportunity to stand in for the pastor in the Sunday pulpit. A granddaughter, also active in her local church, exercises godly influence as a parent and as a teacher in a public school. Another grandson is actively involved in the business world and in his local church, serving as a youth worship leader and deacon. All of their spiritual lives have been shaped in part by the testimony and legacy of a godly grandfather.

Our family is scattered across a geographic region of well over one hundred thousand square miles. Yet the spiritual influence of grandparents continues to be felt by children, grandchildren, and great-grandchildren. Solomon understood the value of this influence when he wrote in Proverbs 16:31, "Gray hair is a glorious crown; it is found in the way of righteousness."

# CHAPTER TEN

# BE A FAMILY FOR SENIOR ADULTS

*Robert Lee Stanford*

**W**e were a pair well fit. They didn't expect much, and we couldn't provide much. We loved Jesus and we liked to sing, and that was about all we had to offer. So that little country church in deep East Texas was just right for my wife and me to serve as music director and pianist during our university years. I hadn't quite mastered the 4/4 conducting pattern, but I could wave my hands on the beat. My wife was just beginning to get comfortable with "Rock of Ages" in the key of B-flat. Thankfully, we had some help from the church organist. Mrs. Whitten was in her early 70's but she never let one arthritic finger slow her down. She could load that Hammond drawbar organ with tremolo and make it "walk and talk." The tremolo was so heavy some Sundays that, when we sang "Rock of Ages," only the most attuned could discern whether we were calling the people to worship or beginning a funeral march.

During one holiday season, my wife and I couldn't go home, and Mrs. Whitten couldn't share the holiday with her daughter and grandchildren either, so she invited us over for a special meal. I will never forget what she said to me, "Since my grandchildren are too busy to come and get me, I'll just be your grandmother." For two years she became a combination mother, grandmother, and best friend for us. That close relationship ended when we transitioned to seminary, but she was—for a period of time—what I refer to now as a "surrogate grandparent." Mrs. Whitten was unforgettable; thirty-seven years later, my memory of her still warms my heart and brings a smile to my face.

Do you know anyone who might need a surrogate grandmother or grandfather? Maybe it's a Sunday School member or a choir member. Maybe it's that single lady who sits behind you in worship or that little boy whose disruptive behavior catches your attention. Who do you know that would be helped and encouraged by the ministry of senior adults who could serve as surrogate grandparents? The Bible has much to say about senior citizens and their important place in the family of God.

## SO WHAT'S THE PROBLEM?
### An Untapped Supply of Wisdom and Service

Surrogate grandparents have a valuable and even irreplaceable role in the immediate and extended church family. Unfortunately, the senior adults who might fulfill this role may remain unnoticed, ignored, or not given due consideration. So what roles do they fill? Is it just hugs, candy, and money for the building fund? If there's more for senior adults to do, what might this look like in a real-life congregation?

Although old age does not automatically qualify one as a mentor, research indicates that "the ideal mentors for younger persons are those of older years with a rich background in worldly experience, acquired skills, character development, personal on-hand resources, numerous contacts, discretionary time, and financial reserves."[47] Our spiritual and moral values come from deep fountains of truth and practices that have been shaped by the Word of God. Every Christian generation has the responsibility to pass on this reservoir of truth. There are few people more qualified to pass on truth to the next generation than our senior adults who have seen

"God, You have taught me from my youth, and I still proclaim your wonderful works. Even when I am old and gray, God, do not abandon me. Then I will proclaim Your power to another generation, Your strength to all who are to come" (Psalm 71:17–18).

the results of these sacred truths lived out in their world. Our seniors who have loved the Lord may enrich the rest of us with a sense of continuity that connects us with previous generations. Simply put, a faithful senior adult knows that the Word of God works! They have experienced it first-hand. These folks have witnessed and experienced blessings and discipline according to their own or others' responses to God's Word. Do you see how valuable a senior adult ministry can be—not merely a ministry *for* seniors, but ministry *by* seniors?

## HOW DOES GOD'S WORD PROVIDE A NEW POSSIBILITY?

### The Bible and Older Adults

The Bible is far from silent when it comes to older adults. The apostle Paul gives Grandma Lois her fair share of credit for Timothy's spiritual formation (2 Timothy 1:5). The Bible records the lives of Moses, Joshua, and Caleb and recognizes that it was in their older years that their faithfulness came to full fruition. Paul writes in Titus 2:3, perhaps thinking of the wholesome examples he had witnessed in Lois and Eunice, "In the same way, older women are to be reverent in behavior, not slanderers, not addicted to much wine. They are to teach what is good."

The senior citizens in our churches are a dynamic and important group. Whether one is seventeen or seventy, we are all made in the *image of God*, even if it is a scarred image. Each senior adult maintains his or her value as a person because he was created by and for God.[48] It is our personhood that reflects the *image of God* in a number of ways including, having an "orientation towards understanding about what is right and wrong, good and bad, worthy and unworthy, just and unjust."[49] As a person increases in years, we must not assume he or she decreases in personhood, dignity, and value.

According to Numbers 3, Moses was eighty years old when he began the monumental task of leading the exodus of God's people from Egypt. No matter how you slice it, eighty is way past adolescence and the exodus movement was not the relocation of just a handful of settlers! God chose a man of years to do the work of a lifetime.

In Joshua 13, we are told that "Joshua was now old, getting on in years, and the LORD said to him, 'You have become old, getting on in years, but a great deal of the land remains to be possessed.'" (Joshua 13:1). It sounds as though God is about to suggest that Joshua retire, *"You are old. There is still a great deal to do. Go home, put your feet up."* But "old and advanced" Joshua still had extraordinary challenges ahead of him! Eleven chapters later, after the land is conquered and fully divided, Joshua 24:29 concludes, "After these things, the LORD's servant, Joshua son of Nun, died at the age of 110." Even while Joshua was multiplying in years, he was dividing the conquered land among the people.

And how about Caleb? One day Caleb and Joshua had a talk. This was not one of the old-timers' gabfests so often pictured of older people. This was a birthday conversation that had to do with forging the future:

> As you see, the LORD has kept me alive these 45 years as He promised, since the LORD spoke this word to Moses while Israel was journeying in the wilderness. Here I am today, 85 years old. I am still as strong today as I was the day Moses sent me out. My strength for battle and for daily tasks is now as it was then. Now give me this hill country the LORD promised me on that day, because you heard then that the Anakim are there, as well as large fortified cities. Perhaps the LORD will be with me and I will drive them out as the LORD promised" (Joshua 14:10-12).

Obviously Caleb was not in a retirement mode. At eighty-five years old Caleb was dreaming about the next eighty-five years. Seniors like Moses, Joshua, and Caleb continued to take on challenges, to accomplish great feats, and to influence the next generation even into their latter years.

## SURROGATE GRANDPARENTS AND FAMILY MINISTRY

Many children in your church probably do not have a grandparent nearby. While the technological world has made incredible advancements in connecting people, social media and live-streaming videos can never replace or reproduce a grandmother's love or a grandfather's presence. Some children do not even know their grandparents. So how can the older folks in our churches minister to the church family? Let's consider a few ideas together.

| FAMILY MINISTRY PRIORITIES | APPLICATIONS FOR OLDER ADULTS |
|---|---|
| Surrogate Grandparenting | An organized ministry that seeks to connect families who need the presence of a grandparent figure in their lives could be significant for both the surrogate grandparent and the young family. <ul><li>How about a stand-in grandmother who spends time with a single mom each week? What if this grandmother attended an occasional parent-teacher conference or special school events while mom is working?</li><li>What about an older couple who invites a single parent and children over for dinner once a month? The stories that an older adult can tell might amaze even the most jaded pre-teen.</li><li>How about assigned surrogate grandparents who sit with children while their parents sing in the choir? In this way, older adults can become honorary choir members without ever singing a note!</li><li>What if an older adult couple watched a child once each month to provide a date night for a younger couple that needs some free time to communicate with each other?</li></ul> |

| FAMILY MINISTRY PRIORITIES | APPLICATIONS FOR OLDER ADULTS |
|---|---|
| **Practical Mentoring from One Generation to the Next** | A mentoring ministry for those who are on their way to senior adult status can be helpful as well. Most of us will be grandfathers and grandmothers someday. Yet, unless you are on the verge of retirement, you might not be thinking about these future years. Who is better equipped than senior adults to teach, counsel, and warn about the pearls and perils of retirement and grandparenthood?<br><br>• Senior adults could offer retirement workshops and seminars and even help to develop resource materials.<br>• Senior adults can meet with young or midlife couples and offer step-by-step assistance in preparing for retirement, even helping those nearing retirement to understand programs like Medicare and Medicaid. These seniors will speak candidly about things they did right as well as cautioning about what they did wrong in retirement preparation. Such workshops can have a positive effect on family and individual stewardship, particularly when it comes to giving.<br>• Senior adults could meet with recently-married couples in the church once each month to talk about ways to strengthen marriages in each stage of life. |
| **Volunteer Service Partnerships for Senior Adults** | Consider developing a senior adult organization that supports and assists other programs in the church and community. Some churches have dubbed this group of senior adults "the LLL Club": Live Long and Like it! This ministry is a means for training and organizing volunteers. Make contact with your local Chamber of Commerce, care centers, school system, after-school programs, crisis pregnancy centers, adoption agencies, or other worthy community organizations, requesting a list of volunteer needs. Enlist and train senior adults to serve these needs. Celebrate these seniors' service by thanking them in worship services or by recognizing them in Sunday School classes and community groups. |

## GRANDPARENTS, SPECIALLY GIFTED TO BE FAMILY MINISTERS

Some folks were way ahead of their time when it comes to family ministry.

Go back with me to a small town Texas town in the 1970s and a surrogate grandmother named Fannie. Fannie wore her gray hair in a bun that looked like a long-abandoned beehive. She was missing most of her front teeth. Her voice was strained and tight but her words were always pleasant. If I recall rightly, she always walked to church in the same full-flowing housedress. As much as she boasted about other people's children, I never remember her speaking of her own. Perhaps she never had any.

Despite these many disadvantages, Fannie had something special. She had a church family that adored her. We loved her and trusted her, and she became everyone's granny. How? She served in the nursery. She gave wise advice and encouragement to young moms. Young men and older men alike would stand in line to get a hug from Fannie. On one particular occasion the church honored her as "everyone's grandma." Fannie left a legacy of love and ministry. She taught us that seniors are specially gifted to be family ministers.

Surely there are many in our churches who could become just like her! Will you give them an opportunity to serve? Will you help them to see that it is indeed "more blessed to give than to receive"? (Acts 20:35). Will you equip your congregation to hear their voices and to value their wisdom?

# DEVELOPING A
# D6 VISION

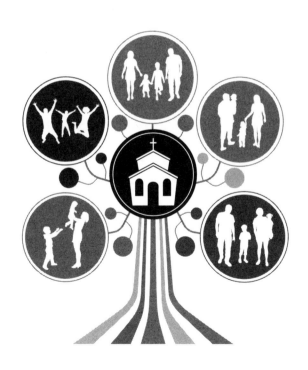

# CHAPTER ELEVEN

# DEVELOPING A
# D6 VISION FOR
# OUR FAMILIES:

*Parenting from the Perspective
of a Story That's Bigger Than Me*[50]

*Timothy Paul Jones*

At the center of God's work with humanity stands this singular act: In Jesus Christ, God personally intersected human history and redeemed humanity at a particular time in a particular place. Yet this central act of redemption does not stand alone. It is bordered by God's good creation and humanity's fall into sin on the one hand and by the consummation of God's kingdom on the other.

This divine storyline of creation, fall and law, redemption, and consummation is the story that Christians have repeated to one another and to the world ever since Jesus ascended into the sky and sent His Spirit to dwell in His first followers' lives. This age-old plot line should frame every aspect of our lives—including how we treat and train children. To have a biblical worldview is to interpret every aspect of our lives—including our relationships with children—within the framework of this singularly glorious story.

# GIFTS FROM GOD AND SINNERS IN NEED

In each movement of God's storyline, it is clear that children are neither burdens to be avoided nor byproducts of human sin. Every child is a blessing and a gift (Psalm 127:3–5). Even before humanity's fall into sin, God designed the raising of children to serve as a means for the multiplication of His manifest glory around the globe (Genesis 1:26–28). A few bites of forbidden fruit, raising Cain as well as Abel, and a worship service that ended in fratricide took their toll on that first family—but God refused to give up on His first purpose to turn the family into a means for revealing His glory. God promised that, through the offspring of Eve, He would send a Redeemer to fulfill His plan to pour out His glory over all the earth (Genesis 3:15; 4:1, 25). In a pattern that persists throughout Scripture, the family becomes a path both for bringing the Messiah into the world and for passing the message of the Messiah from one generation to the next.

After the fall, men and women still exercise divinely ordered dominion over God's creation by raising children (Genesis 1:26-28; 8:17; 9:1-7; Mark 10:5-9). What has changed in the aftermath of the fall is that children have become not only gifts to be nurtured, but also sinners to be trained. And yet, in all of this, the family remains a *means* in God's plan, never the goal and never the source or center of our identity.

1. **In a biblical worldview, the training of children is a primary parental responsibility:** Parents possess a responsibility not only to provide their children's needs but also to train their children to reflect God's glory. This doesn't release the larger community of faith from a responsibility for shaping children's souls. The Great Commission to "make disciples" was given to the whole people of God and includes every age group (Matthew 28:19). Neither does this mean that parents must be the sole instructors in their children's lives. Parents may partner with church ministries or enlist schools to develop certain skills in their children's lives— but parents still bear final responsibility before God for how their children are trained for life.

In the Old Testament, Moses commanded parents—and particularly fathers—to train their children in God's ways (the pronouns translated "you" and "your" in Deuteronomy 6:6-7 are masculine singular in the original language). Moses expected children to ask their parents about their family's spiritual practices, and he prepared fathers to respond in ways that highlighted God's mighty works (Exodus 12:25-28; Deuteronomy 6:20-25). These expectations persisted throughout Israel's songs and early history (Joshua 4:6; Psalm 78:1-7). This ancient heritage of songs, statutes, and ceremonies foreshadowed the coming of Jesus and explicitly recognized the primacy of parents in their children's training.

Paul reiterated this point in the New Testament when he reminded fathers to nurture their children in the "training and instruction of the Lord" (Ephesians 6:4). Paul seems to have derived this phrase from Deuteronomy 11:2, where "discipline of the LORD" prefaced a description of how God disciplined His people to remind them of His covenant with them. In other letters, Paul applied these same two terms—*training* and *instruction*—to patterns that characterized the disciple-making relationships of Christian brothers and sisters. *Training* implied discipline and described one of the key results of training in the words of God (2 Timothy 3:16). *Instruction* included warnings to avoid unwise behaviors and ungodly teachings (1 Corinthians 10:11; Titus 3:10). Such texts strongly suggest that Paul was calling parents—and particularly fathers—to do far more than manage their children's behaviors and provide for their needs. Paul expected parents to train their children to engage with their world in light of God's words and God's ways.

2. **In a biblical worldview, the training of children is worldview training.** This training includes far more than merely increasing children's biblical knowledge or involving them in a community

of faith. Moses commanded the Israelites to teach their offspring to view all they did ("hands") and all they chose ("forehead"), as well as how they lived at home ("doorposts") and how they conducted business ("your gates") within the all-encompassing framework of a God-centered worldview (Deuteronomy 6:8-9). "Wisdom" in Proverbs was conveyed from father to child and included not only knowledge about God, but also practical skills for engaging with the world in light of God's truth. Skills in craftsmanship, leadership, and a broad range of other fields all fell under the heading of wisdom, which begins with "the fear of the Lord" (Exodus 31:3, 6; Deuteronomy 34:9; Proverbs 1:7). Persons outside the believing community may possess these skills, but only the believer sees them as God intended, as signposts pointing to the order and glory of God. There is no biblical warrant for separating the training of children into "secular" and "sacred" categories, with one handled by the world and the other superintended by parents. God is Lord over all of life.

3. **In a biblical worldview, the training of children includes formal and informal components.** Moses commanded the Israelites not only to teach God's words to their children, but also to discuss these truths informally throughout each day (Deuteronomy 6:7-9). In Proverbs, the father passed on particular teachings to his son (Proverbs 4:2), but he also provided occasional instructions in response to specific situations (Proverbs 4:1)—once again, a combination of formal and informal components. The biblical pattern is for both parents to be involved in these practices of formal and informal training. The book of Proverbs specifically mentions the mother's role five times (Proverbs 1:8, 4:3, 6:20, 31:1, 26). According to biblical scholar Peter Gentry, this inclusion of the mother is unparalleled in the wisdom literature of the Ancient Near Eastern nations that surrounded Israel.[51] The father possessed a particular responsibility to lead, but the father's responsibility did not negate or diminish the mother's supportive role in the nurture and admonition of children.

## YOUR CHILD IS FAR MORE THAN YOUR CHILD

Viewed from the vantage of creation and fall, children are both gifts to be treasured and sinners to be trained. Yet no amount of training can ever raise a child to the level of God's perfect righteousness. And even the best training may not result in a child's perseverance in the faith; the popular text that declares "even when he is old he will not depart" is not an airtight promise to parents but a proverb—a pithy observation about how life typically works (Proverbs 22:6).

Every order of creation, including our training of children, has been subjected to frustration with the gap between the glory of God's creation and the fact of humanity's fallenness (Romans 8:20-22). The ultimate answer to this gap is not better education but a perfect substitute—and that is precisely what God provided in Jesus Christ. Through Christ, God bridged the gap between His perfection and humanity's imperfection (2 Corinthians 5:21). The death of Jesus brought about the possibility of redemption in the present; His resurrection guaranteed the consummation of God's kingdom in the future.

This truth introduces a radical new dimension to how we view children. To embrace God's redemption is to be adopted in Jesus Christ as God's heir, gaining a new identity that transcends every earthly status (Romans 8:15-17; Galatians 3:28-29; 4:3-7; Ephesians 1:5; 2:13-22). As a community united in Christ, the church becomes the believer's first family. "Whoever does the will of my Father in heaven, that person is My brother and sister and mother," Jesus said (Matthew 12:50). Paul made much the same point when he directed Timothy to encourage "younger men as brothers" and "younger women as sisters" (1 Timothy 5:1-2). Because the church is a family, in instances where one parent is absent or an unbeliever, other believers may become that child's parents in the faith (2 Timothy 1:2, 5; 3:15).

What this means for followers of Jesus is that every child is far more than a child. Every child is first and foremost a potential or actual brother or sister in Christ. Whatever children stand beside us in eternal glory will not stand beside us as our children or as our students. They will stand beside us because and only because they have become our brothers and sisters, "heirs of God and coheirs with Christ" (Romans 8:17; see also Galatians 4:7; Hebrews 2:11; James 2:5; 1 Peter 3:7).

Every child is an eternal soul whose days will long outlast the rise and fall of all the kingdoms of the earth. They, their children, and their children's children will flit ever so briefly across the face of this earth before being swept away into eternity (James 4:14). If these children become our brothers and sisters in Christ, their days upon this earth are preparatory for glory that will never end (Daniel 12:3; 2 Corinthians 4:17–5:4; 2 Peter 1:10-11). That's why our primary purpose for the children that we educate in our churches and homes must not be anything as small and miserable as earthly success. Our purpose should be to leverage children's lives to advance God's kingdom so every tribe, every nation, and every people-group gains the opportunity to respond in faith to the rightful King of kings.

# CHAPTER TWELVE

# DEVELOPING A D6 VISION FOR OUR MINISTRY:

*When God Speaks Through Google*

*Philip L. McKinney II*

I still remember when it happened—that moment when God slapped me across the face with a message I needed to hear.

Before I explain the message I needed to hear, I need to explain my context at the time. I have been ministering to students and their families for more than two decades in both vocational and volunteer ministry. When I first entered into youth ministry, I thought it was the greatest job in the world. After all, what's *not* to like about planning activities and going on fun trips all the time and all somehow pleasing God in the process? I grew up in the midst of the heyday of event-driven youth ministry. To a young man wanting to serve the Lord, but with a large side order of selfishness, it was the ideal job. I remember going to college and reading all the books on how to plan the next "wow-them" event. Each event attracted greater and greater numbers of teens—but many of these teens were drawn closer to me and further away from their parents. Honestly, that boosted this young man's pride.

For about a decade, I was living the student ministry dream. Unfortunately, it was becoming increasingly clear that the teens graduating from my ministry were unable to find their place in the multigenerational community of faith. Church leaders began to ask questions about my efforts and tactics and wanted answers. A ministry that had been vaunted as a highly successful youth ministry was forced to redefine success in terms of something other than numbers.

I added a few family events, but parents still seemed to rely on me to shape their children's souls. And why shouldn't they? I'd spent several years pretending that I was the church's professional disciple-maker for students!

That's when it happened.

God spoke to me through Google.

I was away from the office for a day of prayer and focus. I laid all of this before the Lord as a servant who had lost his way. I repented of my self-seeking and sincerely begged God for a new direction. I don't recall exactly what search terms I entered into Google, but the first thing that popped up on the screen was "the *Shema*." I had a clear sense from God's Spirit that this was to be my guide.

The *Shema*, I recalled, was the statement of faith that appeared in Deuteronomy 6. It wasn't that I had never heard of this text. I had studied it and even preached it—but I don't know that the words had ever infiltrated my heart until that moment when the Spirit clearly conveyed that this text would become my guide. I believe these words and their immediate context should shape our approach to spiritual formation in both the physical and spiritual family. My premise is that spiritual formation is a team effort, which includes both the church and the family with the primary responsibility resting in the hands of parents.

## THE LORD OUR GOD

At the very root of all Scripture is one basic principle: There is one God, and you are not Him. From the beginning, humanity has struggled with the concept that God is God, and we are not.

When Satan entered the picture he introduced a question into the minds of Adam and Eve (Genesis 3:1), "Did God really say . . .?" Up until this point in the history of humankind, we have no record of any doubt or questioning. What we see instead is humankind basking in the glory of God, living daily in the presence of pure love. Yet when faced with the question, "Did God really say . . . ?" humankind begins to question God. Satan even introduces the lie that will plague humankind for all time, "You will *be like God*" (Genesis 3:5, emphasis mine). It is at this moment that humankind not only questions God, but also longs to be God.

Fast-forward to the time of the Exodus. Moses declares, "Listen, Israel: The LORD our God, the LORD is One" (Deuteronomy 6:4). This text is known as the *Shema*—from the Hebrew word that opens the sentence, "Listen." God knows His children's struggles and sets this single truth at the root of all His commands, "I'm God and you're not. There is *no* other." This was and is the most difficult concept for humankind to accept, but it is also the most necessary! As we strive to grow our children and others in the Lord, our starting premise must be, "*God* is *God*, and we are *not*."

Most people wince at the thought of studying the book of Leviticus because of all its laws and regulations. But this book only seems boring because we miss the beautiful message woven forty-nine times throughout the text: "I am the LORD."[52] Do you think the writer was trying to make a point by repeating this single phrase seven times seven? God wasn't laying down laws to limit His people's lives. The law was a tutor that trained the people in this truth: "I am the Lord, and you're not. Love me and obey."

With these truths in mind, let's look carefully at Deuteronomy 6 and develop a D6—Deuteronomy 6—vision for our families. The text states, "The Lord our God" (Deuteronomy 6:4). These words were spoken in a community and for the sake of a community. This community included families as a basic building block of society, but the vision is broader than any one family.

## WHOLLY LIVING

Once God reminded His children that He alone was God, He made clear *how* He wanted them to love Him: He wanted them to love Him *wholly.* "Love the LORD your God with all your heart, with all your soul, and with all your strength" (Deuteronomy 6:5). When questioned about the greatest command, Jesus responded with this one (Matthew 22:37-38; Mark 12:29-30; Luke 10:27). In both Mark and Luke, Jesus is cited as including "mind" in the list of terms and Matthew limits them to "heart," "soul," and "mind." The point of this text is not to list the precise components of a human being, like a list of parts needed for a particular building project. The point is simply that God desires His children to love Him wholly—with all that we are.

We cannot compartmentalize our love and devotion to God. Our love for God must encompass and saturate every aspect of our lives. The Israelites were commanded to do this individually, in the home, and as a part of a greater community. "These words" were to be passed on to all the coming generations so God's people would never forget them.

## REPEAT, TALK, BIND, AND WRITE

God did not leave the Israelites to themselves to figure out how to pass on these words to the next generation.

> These words that I am giving you today are to be in your heart. *Repeat* them to your children. *Talk* about them when you sit in your house and when you walk along the road, when you lie down and when you get up. *Bind* them

as a sign on your hand and let them be a symbol on your forehead. *Write* them on the doorposts of your house and on your gates (Deuteronomy 6:6-9, emphasis mine).

The commands about hands and forehead may have been meant metaphorically—through some Israelites took them quite literally, using leather straps to tie biblical texts on their hands and heads, like ancient predecessors of the WWJD bracelet. But how should we respond to this text? How might we allow God's Word to shape our thoughts and actions—our head and hands—today?

### Repeat

The first directive is to "repeat" or "impress" these words in our children's lives. Some see a connection between this word and an engraver who painstakingly engraves a monument through repeated actions with a hammer and chisel. The engraver etches images and text into the face of the stone. While the task may seem dull and daunting, the result is permanence.[53] If this is true, then how might we "chisel" this message or these words onto the hearts and minds of our children? Meditation and memorization might be two places to start.

When we hear the word meditation, our thoughts sometimes slip into thinking about an orange-robed bald man sitting cross-legged and humming. Biblical meditation, however, is the repetition of God's Word to the point that it is internalized and reshapes the heart, soul, mind, and strength. There are four biblical objectives for meditation:

**Worship:** It is a time to focus on and commune with the Lord and His works (Psalms 27:4; 77:12). It means filtering out distractions so our children can learn to hear God's voice through His written Word. The goal of biblical meditation is to internalize and to personalize Scripture so its truth can affect how we think, feel, act, and live.

**Instruction**: It is a time to better understand God's Word and how it applies to our lives (Psalms 49:3; 119:27, 97f). In meditation we exchange our thoughts with God's thoughts.

**Encouragement:** It is a time to motivate and inspire us in service for the works that God has called us to do (Joshua 1:7-8).

**Transformation:** It is a time when we are receptive to God's transforming work (Psalms 4:4; 19:14; 119:15; Romans 12:2).

Memorization is one result of meditation. As God's Word is repeated over and over, His thoughts are chiseled into the hearts, souls, minds, and strength of our children and us.

### Talk

How many "God-conversations" does a typical family have with their children? Research has shown that parents recognize their role as the spiritual directors of their children, but most do not have regular conversations about how God's truth applies in their daily lives.[54] It is crucial that parents not only understand the necessity of God-conversations, but also that they know how to go about it. Many of our parents simply lack a confidence when it comes to how to start a conversation about God with their children.

I can remember God-conversations with my dad growing up. They primarily took place in the evenings before bed or in the truck going to work, although my dad talked about God constantly. I can vividly remember our nightly ritual of dad sitting on our beds and reading God's Word to us. He would then discuss with us what that means to our lives. My dad was a carpenter by trade, and he brought me up in that trade as well. Every summer I worked alongside my dad building homes. I remember how I would wake up each morning to find my dad sitting at the table with his pipe in one hand and his Bible in the other. He would begin his day with his Father and would then talk with me about what he had just read. All of those experiences shaped my life-long commitment to the Lord and to ministry.

One way in which I have tried to mimic this in my life with my kids is to sing the *Shema* before bed each night. Now, I must admit that I don't always remember to do this, but my children have a way of reminding me now because it has become a part of their "routine," which will be remembered down the road. These conversations should be when you rise and when you go to bed; when you go out for pizza and on the way to a ball game. They should take place in the daily routine of life and the set times you coordinate in your families. There are many other ways to do this, but the point is to be intentional and consistent.

### Bind

Today, we may reminisce about the WWJD bracelets and even joke about them. Yet are there ways that we might wear God's Word wherever we go? Are there ways we can help our children learn God's Word simply by placing a hand-written Scripture in their lunch box or writing Scriptures on post-it notes and placing them in areas where our teenagers spend a lot of time? (If you have teenage girls, the bathroom mirror would be a great spot to start!) Are we intentional about these things, or are we simply trusting that our children see plenty of Scripture by showing up at church each week?

### Write

How about the simple task of writing down God's Word together? What if we made a habit of writing out different passages of God's Word as a part of our family devotions? Maybe Scripture would begin to take root, and His Words would flow from our hearts and mouths because it is constantly in our thoughts and on our pages.

## IMPLICATIONS FOR SPIRITUAL FORMATION

Spiritual formation is not the sole responsibility of parents or the church. It is a team effort that requires intentionality on both parts without the exclusion of one or the other. The context of the *Shema* teaches that both parents and the community of believers are responsible for passing on the faith.[55] Spiritual formation should not be left to chance and should be intentional on the part of parents *and* the church. The two cannot be mutually exclusive, but must work together to set children and teens on the path toward spiritual maturity. It cannot be assumed that children will simply gain a biblical Christian worldview simply because they have Christian parents. Instead, the church must be intentional about educating and equipping parents to do their God-ordained work while coming alongside them in the process with opportunities to further spiritual formation in their children and teens in the context of the church.

But, of course, we never stop with Deuteronomy 6, because God didn't stop with Deuteronomy 6! Every syllable of the Old Testament has a goal greater than the law, and that greater goal is the kingdom of God in Christ. Jesus Christ "is the focus of every single word of the Bible. Every verse of Scripture finds its fulfillment in him, and every story in the Bible ends with him."[56] A Christ-centered D6 vision refuses to burden families with the condemnation that grows from a focus on the law that none of us can keep. Instead, this vision turns families toward our elder brother who kept the law in our place (Hebrews 2:11-15)—toward Jesus Christ who is, even now, forming everyone who finds their rest in Him into a new family, "a chosen race, a royal priesthood, a holy nation, a people for his possession" (1 Peter 2:9). It's only through him that our vision for the discipleship of the next generation can produce transformation that lasts beyond the generations, into a kingdom that never ends.

# ACKNOWLEDGEMENTS

This book began soon after I (Timothy) finished the first draft of *Family Ministry Field Guide.* I was teaching a doctoral seminar at the time, and I asked the students to read and to critique my manuscript. Several of them were pastors and wondered if I planned to add an appendix to *Family Ministry Field Guide* with specific ideas and activities to incorporate into a family-equipping church. Such an appendix would have made *Family Ministry Field Guide* longer than I wanted—but I agreed that such a resource might be worthwhile.

That's when some students began to share ideas from their own ministries—and most of them were great ideas! We laughed as John Steen told us about the Steen Family Bible Hour and Steve Wright described how a parent wanted a child to give a testimony, but instead the child described how he recently began using the toilet for the first time. (Steve also regaled us with completely unrelated stories about how he blew up a gas station and switched his grandfather's false teeth with a goat's teeth; regrettably, we were unable to find a spot for those stories in this book.) As we shared ministry ideas, we began to talk about developing those ideas into a book. We decided that—if a book did develop from this discussion—royalties from the book would be given away. Thus, this book was born.

Once the chapters were completed, doctoral student Christopher Harding edited the entire manuscript. Mike Nappa of Nappaland Literary Agency worked with Randall House to direct all royalty proceeds from this book to Bethany Christian Services in Indianapolis and Louisville. By purchasing this book, you have supported efforts to end abortion by caring for the physical and spiritual needs of women who are facing unplanned pregnancies.

Many thanks are due to Ron Hunter for the many opportunities to serve in the D6 Conference, Michelle Orr at Randall House who coached this manuscript to completion, Nick Weyrens who completed the first round of copyediting, Garrick Bailey for administrative support throughout the process, and the leadership and trustees of The Southern Baptist Theological Seminary for their unflagging support of the writing efforts of faculty and students.

*Timothy Paul Jones*
*and John David Trentham*

*Editors*

# CONTRIBUTORS

DANNY R. BOWEN (Ph.D., The Southern Baptist Theological Seminary) is adjunct professor of Christian ministry at The Southern Baptist Theological Seminary. He and his wife enjoy grandparenting and traveling. Danny is also a nurse anesthetist and has authored textbook chapters in *Nurse Anesthesia* (Saunders) and *Obstetric Anesthesia* (Lippincott).

SCOTT DOUGLAS (Ed.D., The Southern Baptist Theological Seminary) is the student minister at Westside Baptist Church in Murray, Kentucky. He enjoys spending time with his wife and two boys, reading, and writing for building leaders in the church. Scott is the author of *Dream Teams* (Rainer), and he has published articles in *Canyon Journal of Interdisciplinary Studies* and *Journal of Applied Christian Leadership*.

CHRISTOPHER HARDING (Ph.D., The Southern Baptist Theological Seminary) is family pastor at First Baptist Church, Lenoir City, Tennessee. He, his wife, and their two children like music, mission trips, and really good pizza.

BRIAN HOWARD HONETT (M.Div., The Southern Baptist Theological Seminary) is a chaplain in The United States Air Force. He, his wife, and their six children love sports, barbecue, and building with Legos.

TIMOTHY PAUL JONES (Ph.D., The Southern Baptist Theological Seminary) is associate vice president and C. Edwin Gheens

Professor of Christian Family Ministry at The Southern Baptist Theological Seminary, where he teaches in the areas of family ministry and applied apologetics. Before coming to Southern, he led churches in Missouri and Oklahoma as pastor and associate pastor. Dr. Jones has authored or contributed to more than a dozen books, including *PROOF; Conspiracies and the Cross; Perspectives on Family Ministry*; and, *Christian History Made Easy.* In 2010, Christian Retailing magazine selected *Christian History Made Easy* as the book of the year in the field of Christian education. He is married to Rayann and they have three daughters. The Jones family serves in SojournKids children's ministry at Sojourn Community Church.

GARY MAY (Ph.D., The Southern Baptist Theological Seminary) serves as the senior pastor of Trinity Baptist Church of Longview, Texas. He, with his wife Carolyn, enjoys riding motorcycles, spending time with their two grandchildren, and teaching at the university level.

PHILIP L. MCKINNEY II (Ph.D., The Southern Baptist Theological Seminary) is a minister of discipleship in northern Virginia and serves as adjunct professor at Harding University and Toccoa Falls College. Phil loves spending his time with his wife and three daughters. He has written for *Journal of Biblical Perspectives in Leadership* and *Journal of Discipleship and Family Ministry.*

JOSHUA A. REMY (M.Div., The Southern Baptist Theological Seminary) lives in Columbus, Ohio, with his wife and three daughters. He is a pastor serving with Veritas Community Church and also works and ministers in real estate and teaching.

ROBERT (BOB) LEE STANFORD (Ph.D., The Southern Baptist Theological Seminary) serves as pastor of Comal Church. He and his wife enjoy their two sons, four grandsons, and daughter-in-love, as well as Buddy the family mutt.

JOHN ELLIS STEEN (Ph.D., The Southern Baptist Theological Seminary) is middle school pastor at Long Hollow Baptist Church. John loves to spend time with students having fun and telling them that God loves them. He and his wife Jennifer have three children. His favorite place to go grab a burger is Five Guys Burgers and Fries.

MATTHEW SCOTT THOMPSON (M. Div., The Southern Baptist Theological Seminary) is associate pastor for worship and family ministry at Bloomfield Baptist Church. He is married to Torey, and together they have two children, Ezekiel and Esther.

JOHN DAVID TRENTHAM (Ph.D., The Southern Baptist Theological Seminary) is the Assistant Professor of Leadership and Discipleship, and director of the Doctor of Education Program at the Southern Baptist Theological Seminary. Prior to joining the faculty at Southern Seminary, Dr. Trentham served for several years as the Young Adults & Missions Pastor and Worship Leader at the First Baptist Church of Mount Washington, Kentucky. He is currently an elder at a new church plant in Louisville. He and his wife Brittany are East Tennessee natives and parents of one son, Maddox. Dr. Trentham recently published a major study exploring the nature of development among pre-ministry students attending different types of colleges and universities. He has contributed to academic journals, including *The Journal of Discipleship and Family Ministry*, and is an active member of the Society of Professors in Christian Education.

Steve Wright (Ph.D., The Southern Baptist Theological Seminary) is pastor of discipleship and church planting at Family Church in West Palm Beach, Florida. He has been serving in churches since 1988. He previously served as assistant pastor of student and family ministries at Providence Baptist Church in Raleigh, North Carolina. Steve is the author of *reThink* and *ApParent Privilege* (InQuest). He and his wife Tina have been blessed with three children: Sara, William, and Tyler.

# ENDNOTES

[1]Chap Clark's *The Youth Worker's Handbook to Family Ministry* (Grand Rapids: Zondervan, 1997) was an excellent but overlooked text that I didn't discover until a decade after it was written. For "inclusive-congregational ministry," see Mark Senter III, ed., *Four Views of Youth Ministry and the Church* (Grand Rapids: Zondervan, 2001). The National Center for Family-Integrated Churches began in 2001 with the Summit on Uniting Church and Family.

[2]Charles Sell, *Family Ministry* (Grand Rapids: Zondervan, 1981); Diana Garland, *Family Ministry* (Downers Grove: InterVarsity, 1999).

[3]For more on the origins and development of family life education, see Timothy Paul Jones, "Family Ministry Models," in *A Theology for Family Ministries,* ed. Michael and Michelle Anthony (Nashville: Broadman & Holman, 2011), 171-172. In the first edition of *Family Ministry,* Diana Garland sees her approach as something other than family life education because, in her estimation, family life education deals only with the needs and weaknesses of families, not with their resiliencies and strengths in the context of the community of faith (Diana Garland, *Family Ministry* [Downers Grove: InterVarsity, 1999], 10-11). I would contend that, even in its community-based forms, family life education was never limited in its scope to the needs and weaknesses of families. The key distinguishing dynamic in family life education is not one of basis (need-based *versus* strength-based) but of orientation (orientation toward development of healthier family relationships *versus* orientation toward development of families as contexts for discipleship).

[4]Chronologically and even ideologically, these two expressions of family ministry have, of course, overlapped at times. In the 1990s, Chap Clark and Mark DeVries were emphasizing needed changes that would later become part of the faith-at-home movement at the same time that family life education was flourishing in many churches. Family life education is a real need in churches; my distinction between the two approaches is not intended to denigrate family life education, but simply to demonstrate that the faith-at-home movement is distinct from family life education.

[5]Texts written from a family life education perspective have tended to begin with such topics as "The Family of Family Ministry" or "Families Today," interpreting the family first from the perspective of the latest social-scientific research, identifying such data as the primary means for understanding families and as the foundation for intervening in and changing family and church life (see, e.g., Diana Garland, *Family Ministry* [Downers Grove: InterVarsity Press, 1999], 20).

[6]For the history of family-improvement societies, see M. Lewis-Rowley, et al., "The Evolution of Education for Family Life," in *Handbook of Family Life Education*, Vol. 1: *Foundations of Family Life Education*, ed. M.E. Arcus, et al. (Newbury Park: SAGE, 1993).

[7]For examples of this pattern of faith-at-home developing from disenchantment with previous approaches to youth ministry, see Mark DeVries' *Family-Based Youth Ministry* (Downers Grove: InterVarsity, 1994), Mark Holmen's *Faith Begins at Home* (Bloomington: Bethany House, 2005), Steve Wright's *reThink* (Raleigh: InQuest, 2007), Voddie Baucham's *Family-Driven Faith* (Wheaton: Crossway, 2007), and Brian Haynes' *Shift* (Loveland: Group, 2009). Anecdotally, a group of key faith-at-home leaders—including myself—gathered in 2009. As we talked about the experiences God had used to give us a passion for family discipleship, we recognized all of us were former youth ministers who had arrived at the realization that the youth ministry methods we had formerly followed were fundamentally flawed. "Look at

us!" one individual said. "We're the society of disaffected youth ministers."

8 Eun Sung Roh, "An Analysis of Adoption Ministry Programs for Adoptive Parents in Korean Churches" (Ed.D. thesis, The Southern Baptist Theological Seminary, 2015); Lou Cha, "Towards a Transcultural Model of Family Ministry: Ethnographic Case Studies among Hmong Churches" (Ph.D. prospectus, The Southern Baptist Theological Seminary, 2015); Choong Hyun Lee, "Equipping Parents at Eunhye Korean Presbyterian Church, Indianapolis, Indiana, to be the Primary Disciple Makers of Their Children" (D.Min. project, The Southern Baptist Theological Seminary, 2015).

9 For historical exploration of "church as family," see Joseph Hellerman, *The Ancient Church as Family* (Minneapolis: Augsburg Fortress, 2001). I first heard the term in a lecture by Chap Clark.

10 Jonathan Edwards, "Living to Christ," in *Sermons and Discourses, 1720-1723: Volume 10: The Works of Jonathan Edwards,* ed. W.H. Kimnach (New Haven: Yale University, 1992), 577.

11 Nearly seventy percent of parents in evangelical churches stated that no leader in their church had made any contact with them in the past year regarding how parents might be involved in their children's Christian formation. In another survey, conducted by Barna Research Group, 81% of churched parents placed themselves in a similar category. See Timothy Paul Jones, *Family Ministry Field Guide* (Indianapolis: Wesleyan, 2011), chapter 8, and, "Parents Accept Responsibility for Their Child's Spiritual Development But Struggle With Effectiveness," Barna Research Group, accessed December 13, 2010, http://www.barna.org/barna-update/ article/5-barna-update/120-parents-accept-responsibility-for-their- childs-spiritual-development-but-struggle-with-effectiveness.

12 Bryan Nelson, "The Problem with Family Ministry," in *Trained in the Fear of God,* ed. Randy Stinson (Grand Rapids: Kregel Academic, 2011). For the term "church as first family," see Rodney Clapp,

*Families at the Crossroads* (Downers Grove: InterVarsity, 1993), chapter 4.

[13]Donald S. Whitney, *Family Worship in the Bible, in History, and in Your Home* (Shepherdsville: The Center for Biblical Spirituality, 2005), 3-4.

[14]Results of this survey may be found in Timothy Paul Jones, *Family Ministry Field Guide* (Indianapolis: WPH, 2011).

[15]Randy Stinson and Timothy Paul Jones, *Trained in the Fear of God.* Robert Plummer "Bring them up in the Discipline and Instruction of the Lord: Family Discipleship among the First Christians." (Grand Rapids: Kregel, 2011), 100.

[16]http://www.vincelombardi.com/quotes.html.

[17]Cos H. Davis, Jr., *Children and the Christian Faith, 2nd ed* (Nashville: Broadman Press, 1990), 19.

[18]Art Murphy, *The Faith of a Child* (Chicago: Moody Press, 2000), 37.

[19]Daniel O. Aleshire, *Faith Care: Ministering to All God's People through the Ages of Life* (Philadelphia: Westminster John Knox Press, 1988), 15, 104.

[20]Eugene Chamberlain, *When can a Child Believe?* (Nashville: Broadman Press, 1973), 33.

[21]Timothy Paul Jones, *Perspectives on Family Ministry,* (Nashville: B&H Publishing, 2009), 143.

[22]Charles M. Sell, *Family Ministry* (Grand Rapids: Zondervan, 1995), 132.

[23]Jones, *Perspectives on Family Ministry,* 157.

[24]Eugene H. Merrill, *The New American Commentary: Deuteronomy,* (Nashville: B&H Publishing, 1994), 167.

[25]Historical summary drawn from Marcia Bunge. "Biblical and theological perspectives on children, parents, and 'best practices' for faith formation: resources for child, youth, and family ministry today." (*Dialog* 47, 2008), Hans H. Wiersma. "Law and Gospel, and youth and family ministry." (*Dialog* 47, 2008), and Jones, *Perspectives on Family Ministry.*

[26]Leon Morris, "The Gospel According to Matthew," *The Pillar New Testament Commentary,* (Grand Rapids: William B. Eerdmans Publishing Company, 1992), 659.

[27]Joel B. Green, "The Gospel of Luke," *The New International Commentary on the New Testament,* (Grand Rapids: William B. Eerdmans Publishing Company, 1997), 246.

[28]S. S. Bartchy, "Table Fellowship," *The Dictionary of Jesus and the Gospels,* (Downers Grove: InterVarsity, 1992), 800.

[29]Green, 364.

[30]"Short-term missions, as they are currently being practiced, are creating very little lasting positive change in the participants— whether North Americans, Hondurans, or Kenyans. While the short-term mission trip is often a mountaintop experience for the participants, a few weeks or months later their good intentions to raise money for world missions, work for social justice or deepen their faith have not been translated into actions. If we hope to see those good intentions translated into accomplishments something needs to change. Our own experiences and extensive research on goal-setting theory and social support networks provide us with strong evidence on how short-term missions should be changed. Participants will be much more likely to change their lives in lasting ways if they set specific, demanding and public goals and then are regularly held accountable and encouraged to put them into practice" (Kurt Alan Ver Beek, "Lessons from the Sapling: Review of Quantitative Research on Short-term Missions," in *Effective Engagement in Short-term Missions,* ed. Robert Priest [Pasadena: William Carey, 2012]). For the most comprehensive

work on how to plan short-term mission trips in a manner that produces lasting change in participants, see Michael S. Wilder and Shane Parker, *Transformission* (Nashville: B&H, 2010).

[31]Timothy Paul Jones, *The Family Ministry Field Guide* (Indianapolis: WPH, 2011).

[32]Michael S. Wilder, "Building Missional Families," in *Trained in the Fear of God*, ed. Randy Stinson and Timothy Paul Jones (Grand Rapids: Kregel, 2011).

[33]For 81 percent of parents never having been acknowledged or contacted regarding their children's spiritual development, see "Parents Accept Responsibility for Their Child's Spiritual Development But Struggle With Effectiveness," Barna Research Group, accessed December 13, 2010, http://www.barna.org/ barna-update/article/5-barna-update/120-parents-accept-responsibility-for-their-childs-spiritual-development-but-struggle-with-effectiveness. For youth ministry values expressed through time and budgets, see Daniel Broyles, "An Analysis of S.B.C. Youth Ministry Programmatic Values Investigated through Financial Expenditures and Ministerial Activities" (Ph.D. diss., The Southern Baptist Theological Seminary, 2009).

[34]Timothy Paul Jones, *The Family Ministry Field Guide* (Indianapolis: WPH, 2011).

[35]J.J. Arnett, *Emerging Adulthood* (New York: Oxford University Press, 2004), 312. See also Christian Smith with Patricia Snell, *Souls in Transition* (New York: Oxford University Press, 2009), 5-7. For the purposes of this chapter, the terms "emerging adult" and "young adult" are synonymous, and, for the most part, pertain to "early" emerging adults, ages 18-23, who are yet single.

[36]Ed Stetzer, Richie Stanley, and Jason Hayes, *Lost and Found* (Nashville: B&H, 2009), 37-38; Thom Rainer and Sam Rainer III, *Essential Church? Reclaiming a Generation of Dropouts* (Nashville: B&H, 2008), 132, 184.

[37]Dick Purnell, "Single Adults in Your Ministry: Why They Stay and Why They Stray," *Pastoral Leadership for Manhood and Womanhood*, ed. Wayne Grudem and Dennis Rainey (Wheaton: Crossway Books, 2002), 106-107.

[38]Some data drawn from Christian Smith with Patricia Snell, *Souls in Transition*, (New York: Oxford University Press, 2009) 280-281; 283-286.

[39]J. Larson, "Understanding Stepfamilies," *American Demographics 14* (1992): 360.

[40]Some content is drawn from David Schrock, "What Does the Bible Say About Divorce?": http://viaemmaus.wordpress.com. Depending on how particular texts are interpreted, divorce may preclude persons from particular areas of service in the church—such as eldership and the diaconate (1 Timothy 3:2, 12)—but not from communion in the church or from every area of service, provided that an individual recognizes and repents of sinful patterns that may have characterized his or her divorce.

[41]Gretchen Goldsmith, "Why Your Church Needs to Reach Out to Divorced People": http://www.gretchengoldsmith.com.

[42]To consider the scope of nonnuclear families in the American context, see Dorothy Ruiz's article entitled, "Changing Roles of African American Grandmothers in Raising Grandchildren," published in *The Western World of Black Studies*, Volume 32, 2008, and also, "Beyond the Nuclear Family" by Vern Bengston published in the *Journal of Marriage and Family*, February 2001. Bengston argues, "family multigenerational relations will be more important in the 21st century for 3 reasons: (a) the demographic changes of population aging, resulting in 'longer years of shared lives' between generations; (b) the increasing importance of grandparents and other kin in fulfilling family functions; (c) the strength and resilience of intergenerational solidarity over time."

[43]See Copen and Silverstein in, "Transmission of Religious Beliefs Across the Generations; Do Grandparents Matter," published in the *Journal for Comparative Family Studies* for a review of literature and theories for the transmission of religious ideals in a multigenerational fashion.

[45]Howard Hendricks notes in his book, *Teaching that Changes Lives* (56), that maximum learning comes from maximum involvement. If grandparents see themselves as teachers in the lives of their grandchildren, the use of music becomes an interactive method of gaining maximum involvement in learning.

[47]Charles, G. Oakes, *Working in the Gray Zone* (Franklin: Providence House Publishers, 2000) p. 53.

[48]Anthony A. Hoekema, *Created in God's Image* (Grand Rapids: Eerdmans, 1986) p. 5.

[49]Christian Smith, *Moral Believing Animals* (Oxford: University Press, 2003) p.8.

[50]Some portions of this chapter will appear in the forthcoming *Holman Worldview Study Bible* (Nashville: Holman, 2018).

[51]Peter Gentry, "Raising Children, the Christian Way," in *Journal of Discipleship and Family Ministry 2* (2012): 99.

[52]See Leviticus 11:44, 45; 18:2, 4, 5, 6, 21, 30; 19:3, 4, 10, 12, 14, 16, 18, 25, 28, 30, 31, 32, 34, 36, 37; 20:7, 8, 24; 21:12, 15, 23; 22:2, 3, 8, 9, 16, 30, 31, 32, 33; 23:22, 43; 24:22; 25:17, 38, 55; 26:1, 2, 13, 44, 45.

[53]Eugene Merrill, *Deuteronomy* (Nashville: Broadman and Holman, 1994), 167.

[54]Research by the Barna Group has demonstrated this in a study they conducted titled, "Parents Accept Responsibility for Their Child's Spiritual Development But Struggle With Effectiveness" in 2003. They found that 85% of parents surveyed believed that they held the primary role of directing the spiritual formation of their children, not the church (Only 11% felt it was the role of the church. Also, 96% of the parents surveyed with children

13-years-old or younger believed they held the primary spiritual formation role) (Barna Research Group [2003], barna.org). This research alone would lead one to believe that things are as they should be. However, further study by the group found that "Most of those parents are willing to let their church or religious center provide all of the direct religious teaching and related religious experiences that their children receive (Ibid.)." They found that parents typically do not spend time discussing religious matters with their children throughout the week (Ibid.). This research is backed by a study conducted earlier of some 8,000 teens that were brought up in both Protestant and Catholic homes. The study found that 10% of these families did not discuss faith issues with any degree of regularity, and in 43% of the homes faith was never discussed (Merton Strommen and Richard Hardel, *Passing on the Faith* [Winona: St. Mary's, 2000], 14).

[55]Brian Haynes says, "Along this path of growth described in the Old Testament, family and religion were not mutually exclusive. In fact, they were inseparable" (Brian Haynes, *Shift* [Loveland: Group, 2009], 41). In a family-equipping model, church and family are co-champions and partners and they coordinate efforts to "raise not just a youth group but a generation that loves God with heart, soul, mind, and strength (Mark 12:28-34)" (Jay Strother, "Family-Equipping Ministry," in *Perspectives on Family Ministry* [Nashville: B&H, 2009], 145). A children's or youth minister may still exist, but with different objectives, partnering with and equipping parents with their God-given task. This model does not forget what Köstenberger posits: "God's express will for his people Israel is still his will for God's people in the church today. Christian parents have the mandate and serious obligation to instill their religious heritage in their children. This heritage centers on the personal experience of God's deliverance from sin and his revelation in the Lord Jesus Christ and his death for us on the cross. Christian parents ought to take every opportunity to speak about these all-important matters with their children and to express and impart to their children personal gratitude for what God has done.

While there may be Christian Sunday school teachers and other significant teachers in a child's life, parents must never go back on their God-given responsibility to be the primary source of religious instruction for their children" (Andreas Köstenberger and David Jones, *God, Marriage, and Family* [Wheaton: Crossway, 2004], 102-103). Rather than usurping the parental role, family-equipping encourages church leaders to engage the parents in their God-given task by teaching and equipping them for that role and partnering with them in the education and activities that will be learned in the ministry of the church.

[56]R. Albert Mohler, *He is Not Silent* (Chicago: Moody, 2008), 96.

# What is D6?

BASED ON DEUTERONOMY 6:4-7

A **conference** for your entire **team**

A **curriculum** for every age at **church**

An **experience** for every person in your **home**

## Connecting
## CHURCH & HOME
### These must work together!

**DEFINE & REFINE** Your Discipleship Plan

# www.d6family.com

# A must for parenting in a digital world

TECH SAVVY PARENTING

NAVIGATING YOUR CHILD'S DIGITAL LIFE

BRIAN HOUSMAN

- Be informed about safety and awareness in online browsing
- Discover truths about Internet pornography and its draw for teens
- Talk with your child about texting and sexting
- Set time limits and restrictions with video games
- Understand the role of social networking in the lives of teens
- Learn to protect your high schooler's online reputation
- And many more issues

## TECH SAVVY PARENTING
### BY BRIAN HOUSMAN

d6family.com

(h) randall house
randallhouse.com
1-800-877-7030